The Ultimate Guide to Successful Nursing Job Interviewing

M. L. Miller

Published by SoaringME Publishing

ISBN-13: 978-1-956874-32-7

CONTENTS

Preface

Dear Reader,

If you're looking to improve your interviewing skills and land your dream nursing job or promotion, you're in the right place. My journey to writing this book began in 1997, when I went to a recruiting firm to have them help me find my next job. The office had a wall full of awards in the lobby, over forty recruiters working in the back, and the owner Larry was full of energy and enthusiasm. Instead of finding me a job with one of their clients, Larry convinced me to work for him as a recruiter. At that time, I did not know much about talent acquisition, recruiting, or interviewing, other than it was part of the process to get a job.

Larry had over two decades of recruiting experience, and I spent a couple of years training at his large and successful firm. While there, I set several production records and made hundreds of hires as I worked on a couple of major expansions for some large organizations. These companies embedded me into their panel interviews and hiring committees so that quick decisions could be made. From the beginning of my career, I saw candidates from their initial resume submission, phone screens, face-to-face interviews, committee feedback and debates on who would be offered the job and getting them started. This foundation of experience and training has been invaluable for the rest of my career.

Over the years I have worked with many wonderful candidates and employers. I've recruited for all types of roles at all levels with both large and small companies. I have seen the differences and similarities in employer hiring processes, and learned what works well for candidates and what does not. In 2009, I began to focus on executive recruiting, but continued to receive requests for help from candidates who were earlier in their careers.

In 2010 I spent a couple of years doing some work with homeless military veterans at a non-profit organization. I taught classes on writing better resumes and how to interview more successfully. This led me to start my company SoaringME to help candidates improve their interviewing skills.

I still primarily work on my executive recruiting, but after years of thinking about it, I've finally written a series of books to share what I've learned about successful interviewing. The advice I offer begins once you've landed an interview through your strong resume, professional social media, or networking. I'll teach you everything I didn't know back in 1997 when I started this journey.

This book includes all the information from my other book ***SoaringME The Ultimate Guide to Successful Job Interviewing,*** with additional content specifically geared towards excelling in interviews for nursing positions.

I hope that you get the job or promotion that you're going after!

M. L. Miller

Founder, SoaringME

If you enjoy this book, please post a review.

Visit

SoaringME.com

for additional resources.

Introduction

In ***SoaringME The Ultimate Guide to Successful Nursing Job Interviewing,*** I provide insights and advice that will increase your success in any job interview process. The information draws from my career in talent acquisition which began in 1997. If you take the time to read it thoroughly, it will increase your probability of receiving a job offer.

For employers, the process of recruiting, hiring, and training new employees is a costly and time-consuming endeavor. Hiring the right people makes the organization more successful, while hiring the wrong one costs more in time, money, and lost productivity. As a result, companies have developed hiring processes that increase their ability to find the best match for their jobs and organization. These processes act as a test, and you'll need to pass that test to receive an offer of employment.

A great analogy for interviewing is to think back to when you were in school and scheduled to take an exam that had a major impact on your final grade. Preparing for those big exams increased the probability of your success, and preparing for the interviews will do the same. These tests will not be the ones where you need to recite the exact correct answer from memory, they are more like giving your answers in essay form and making sure that you include the correct major points. Employers will vary slightly in the way that they test candidates, and of course all companies are less than perfect when hiring or promoting the best candidate.

The most common complaint I've heard from candidates throughout the years revolves around the imperfect nature of hiring processes. Many companies make bad hiring decisions, both when offering the job to the wrong person and when they do not offer it to the right one. You can complain all day, every day about the value of asking certain interview questions or requiring a certain background, but as Albert Einstein once said; *"A man should look for what is, and not for what he thinks should be."*.

Imagine that you own a company, and you lose one third of your newly hired employees within their first year on the job, and half of them within their first two years. There are a variety of reasons why this might happen, a portion of this turnover comes from employee-driven choices and some results from employer actions. In total a significant eighty percent of turnover is attributed to bad hiring decisions. The desire to reduce this negative outcome is why you must go through a series of challenging steps before receiving an offer of employment.

On average Americans change jobs twelve times in their career, the most in the world. While most of those job changes happen earlier in their career, if we look at an average over a forty- or fifty-year span it means that Americans will go through the interview process only once every three to four years. Workers in other countries will tend to interview even less often over their career. To put it simply, many job candidates fail because interviewing is not something they do that often.

Interview questions are designed to uncover the information that the employer needs to determine who the best fit for the job is. Your primary objective during this process is to demonstrate through your answers and actions that you are the best match to their idea of the perfect candidate who they want to hire. While doing this, you also need to gather information about the employer, the job, expectations, company culture, and compensation so that you can make an informed decision on whether this opportunity is a good fit for you. Again, not all companies have figured out their hiring process, so I have included chapters on questions for you to ask them, and employer red flags for you to watch out for.

This book will teach you what the people who will be grading your test are looking for, and what the most successful candidates have done. **None of the following advice is meant for you to be dishonest in your interviews, trick anybody or try to be somebody that you are not.** This book will help you maximize your chances of getting your dream job by focusing your answers on demonstrating the value you will bring to the position that you are interviewing for.

Understanding What Recruiters and Hiring Managers are Looking For

To succeed in any interview process, it is vital to have a comprehensive understanding of what the interviewers are seeking to hire. The foundation of this success lies in spending ample time to grasp as much detail as possible about the ideal profile being sought.

Companies start the hiring process with an outline of the duties that they need completed, and then develop a profile of who they think will be the best employee to do this role. Depending on the organization's size, the hiring manager, Human Resources, Talent Acquisition, upper management, or a combination of these may create this persona. The profile of the optimal hire can be influenced by the hiring manager's personal preferences, the team's current makeup, and qualities of the previous employee.

The profile of the ideal person to hire will include hard skills, soft skills, and personality traits. These characteristics will vary slightly from company to company. There are, however, some qualities that most employers are looking for in a new employee. These attributes may not even be listed in the job advertisement, but they are still things that interviewers are evaluating you on and understanding these hidden traits will give you an advantage over other candidates.

Here are the ten most common universal traits that interviewers are seeking.

1. Competence.
2. Passion for that work.
3. Self-motivation.
4. Works well with others.
5. Effective communication skills.
6. Ability to take responsibility for work and mistakes.
7. Good problem-solving skills.
8. Honesty.
9. Ability to listen and follow directions.

10. Reliability.

To identify the perfect candidate for a job, companies typically have a list of desired qualities and attributes, including educational background, training, experience, and personality traits. These may consist of a college degree, a specific major, certifications, industry experience, knowledge of relevant software programs or programming languages, or other tools required for that role. The personality of the ideal candidate might be that of someone who is coachable, someone who is driven and desires future advancement, a good team player, or someone who can work independently.

The interview process is a series of steps meant to evaluate how well a candidate matches this ideal person. It is even more accurate to describe the processes as being designed to eliminate the candidates who are not a good fit. The job advertisement, the questions asked during the interviews, and the decision of who the job offer will go to are all based on this persona.

Understanding the profile for a job is therefore critical to success, as every company has a preconceived notion of the person they want to hire. The profile is divided into two sides: the skills or experience side and the personality or compatibility with the company culture side. By having a solid grasp of these traits, you can position yourself as the best-suited candidate and increase your chances of securing the job.

Here are the best steps to understanding the ideal profile for a specific job.

1. Research 10-20 job ads for similar jobs. Make a list of the duties required and desired attributes listed in all of these advertisements.

2. Research the backgrounds of employees who are currently in similar roles. Look at 10-20 online profiles and the background they had before being hired for a job like the one you want.

3. Ask contacts in your professional network what they think makes people successful in that job, or if they know what type of candidate that company prefers to hire for that type of role.

4. Compile the attributes that repeatedly show up in your research. This is a great starting point for understanding what the interviewers are going to evaluate you against.

For the job you are interviewing for, review the list of required and desired attributes in the job ad. Companies usually list their most desired trait first, and then in descending order by level of importance. I have included a series of exercises like this one to help you understand the profile of the job that you are interviewing for. The ***COMPANION WORKBOOK The Ultimate Guide to Successful Job Interviewing*** includes exercises that can help you understand what the employer is seeking for the job you're interested in.

Most of your answers and interactions should highlight the areas in your background that relate to this ideal candidate they wish to hire. Make sure not to sidetrack your interviewers with a lot of irrelevant information. For example, a job ad for a nurse or therapist at a skilled nursing facility may list experience in working with elderly patients as a major component. When answering questions during the interviews, you should highlight your experience in this area. A software engineer will often work as part of a team, so you should highlight and demonstrate effective communication skills during interviews for these jobs.

I once worked with a candidate who was interviewing for a Vice President role with a small startup client of mine. Part of the personality profile that the Chief Executive Officer desired was somebody who is assertive and would not hesitate to advance the projects that this employee would be working on. The candidate had the education and experience for the job, therefore they initially seemed like a great match. But then she was very tentative in making her decisions and moved slowly to schedule her second interview. This gave the CEO the impression that she did not match what he was looking for on the personality side of the profile and she was removed from consideration. Had she understood the profile more fully, perhaps that would have changed her behavior, but it’s likely she simply wasn't the right fit to begin with. It's crucial to note that comprehending the optimal profile does not imply that you should pretend to be someone else, but rather showcase how you meet the requirements through your conduct and responses during the interview process.

Nursing Candidate Profiles

The profiles sought for various nursing positions incorporate a blend of education, hands-on experience, and suitability for different healthcare settings.

Certified Nursing Assistants (CNAs), typically require a high school diploma or equivalent and completion of a state-approved CNA program. Employers look for candidates with direct patient care experience, with a preference for those who have completed additional training in areas like CPR and basic life support. In long-term care settings, familiarity with tailored care plans is a big plus.

Licensed Practical Nurses (LPNs) typically need a diploma from an accredited practical nursing program and must pass the NCLEX-PN exam for licensure. Employers value LPNs with hands-on experience, especially in medication administration, wound care, and collaboration with a healthcare team. In hospital settings, exposure to diverse medical cases is desirable, while in outpatient or clinic settings, interpersonal skills, and efficient patient care typically give a candidate an advantage.

Registered Nurses (RNs) often hold a Bachelor of Science in Nursing (BSN) degree, although an Associate Degree in Nursing (ADN) is sometimes acceptable. Many employers prefer BSN-prepared RNs, particularly in hospital settings. RNs should have experience in advanced patient assessment, care planning, and collaboration with interdisciplinary teams. Critical thinking and adaptability are crucial, with experience in emergency situations highly valued.

Advanced Practice Registered Nurses (APRNs), comprising roles such as Nurse Anesthetists, Nurse Midwives, Nurse Practitioners (NPs), and Clinical Nurse Specialists (CNS), typically require a Master of Science in Nursing (MSN) or a related field. Specific educational and licensing requirements vary by role. Employers seek APRNs with years of clinical experience in their specialized area. For example, a Nurse Practitioner may need experience in diagnosing and treating medical conditions, while a Nurse Anesthetist may require substantial experience in anesthesia administration, particularly in surgical or operative settings.

Nurse Managers/Administrators often hold an MSN or an MBA in healthcare management. Employers seek candidates with a background in nursing leadership and several years of experience in managerial roles. In hospital settings, familiarity with budgeting, regulatory compliance, and strategic planning is important. In long-term care facilities, experience in overseeing resident well-being and devising tailored care plans is essential.

Nursing Instructors/Educators typically need an MSN or a Doctor of Nursing Practice (DNP) degree. Employers seek candidates with a strong background in curriculum development and several years of clinical or teaching experience. Adaptability to evolving educational technologies and a passion for teaching the next generation of nursing professionals are invaluable.

Nursing Researchers require advanced degrees (typically a Ph.D. in Nursing or a related field) and a robust background in research design, data analysis, and collaboration with institutions. Employers typically seek candidates with a record of being published and years of experience in nursing research. The ability to navigate ethical considerations in research is critical.

In the landscape of different nursing careers, the profiles sought by employers are shaped not only by the value each role brings to healthcare but also by the makeup of the team, and the setting of the role.

How You Will be Evaluated

Preparation is vital for a successful interview. Candidates who do not prepare for an interview are generally viewed as less professional and less interested in the job, leading to fears of underperformance and short tenures if hired. The most successful candidates plan, understand the profile that the employer wants to hire, organize their thoughts and memories, then relate their skills, experience, and traits to that optimal candidate.

Where the interview questions come from.

After a company has decided upon the perfect candidate that they wish to hire for a position, they use that profile to develop an interview process that will evaluate candidates to see if they are a good match. Interviewers may be experienced enough to ask their own questions, but many will use questions from an interview packet. The best way for you to understand what an interviewer is looking for in your answers is a thought exercise where you imagine being the interviewer who is looking for someone who matches an optimal candidate.

For example, imagine that you're interviewing candidates for a *Director, of Nursing* role. You can apply this same process to prepare for whatever job you're interviewing for.

Here is part of the job advertisement that explains the ideal profile that is being sought.

Primary responsibilities include:

- Collaborating with key stakeholders to devise nursing strategies.
- Planning and integrating diverse nursing programs into project team development plans for all assigned projects.
- Directing the planning and execution of meetings with regulatory agencies, representing the organization as needed.
- Conducting regulatory intelligence activities to stay current on the regulatory landscape and competitor practices.

- Keeping the organization informed about existing and potential regulatory and scientific issues.
- Managing and scrutinizing safety reports and submissions.

Education and Skills Requirements:

- Essential knowledge of the healthcare development process.
- Familiarity with laws and regulations impacting the healthcare industry and regulatory expertise.
- Previous experience working with health regulatory agencies, particularly the FDA or EMA.
- Successful track record in NDA, BLA, or MAA filings.
- Preferred prior management experience, showcasing the ability to lead through collaboration.
- Highly organized with meticulous attention to detail.
- Advanced degree in nursing or a related health field is preferred. A minimum of a B.A. or B.S. in nursing or a health-related field, with 7+ years of regulatory experience for the Director role and 10+ years for the Senior Director role.

- Demonstrated personal leadership and collaboration skills. • Willingness to travel up to 25%.

In this mental exercise you are one of several interviewers. I am providing you with a packet of interview questions to guide you as you interview all the candidates that have been screened by the recruiter. This packet shows each of the traits that we are looking for in the person we hire for this role. Underneath each of these traits there is a list of ten to twenty differently worded questions for you to choose from. These questions are designed to assess the candidate's skills or experience and evaluate their proficiency in that area.

In the job advertisement we list "Planning and integrating diverse nursing programs into project team development plans for all assigned projects." As you prepare to interview these candidates, here is how your packet questions might look for the management experience that we are looking for:

Planning and integrating diverse nursing programs.

Q1: How do you provide feedback to your team regarding the implementation of nursing programs, and how do you ensure accountability?

Q2: Share an experience of a nursing project you spearheaded. What factors contributed to its success?

Q3: Narrate a situation where you influenced team members in the implementation of a nursing program. What was the outcome?

Q4: Discuss a time when you managed a team member facing challenges. How did you address the situation?

Q5: What strategies do you employ for planning and facilitating the professional development of your team members in the nursing field?

Q6: How do you handle conflicts arising among team members during the integration of nursing programs into project plans?

Q7: Describe an instance where you had to make the tough decision of letting a team member go in the context of nursing program development. What were the reasons, and how did they respond?

Q8: Share your approach to motivating individuals within your nursing team.

Q9: Illustrate instances where you effectively delegated responsibilities to team members during the planning and integration of nursing programs.

Q10: Reflect on your most significant management weakness in the context of nursing program development and integration. How do you address or mitigate this weakness?

This will be similar for each of the traits that we are seeking in the person we wish to hire. As part of this process, you may be asked to evaluate some of the traits while we will have the other interviewers focus on other attributes. For each characteristic that you are asked to evaluate, you will choose one of the questions from the list. There may be some overlap where multiple interviewers evaluate the same skill, and the candidate's background may affect the questions asked. If the answer you are given leaves you uncertain about that candidates' strength level for that trait, you should ask another question from that same list.

After each interview, you will be asked to rate the candidates on every skill that you were asked to evaluate. In the packet you've been provided, there will typically be some sort of scale to use, such as rate the candidate from 1-5 or rate them as Very Poor, Poor, Adequate, Strong, or Very Strong.

Again, this is a mental exercise that will help you understand where your interviewer is coming from. In addition to the hard skills, I want you to evaluate how long it will take each candidate to become a highly contributing member of our team.

You are also being asked to evaluate the personality fit of each candidate; can you picture them working well with you and others at this company, will they be a hard worker, easy to manage, and will they fit well within our company culture?

After you have spoken with all the candidates we are considering, you will compare them to one another in a feedback meeting with all the other interviewers who met with these same candidates. During this meeting you will likely be asked for your recommendations on which candidates to move forward in the process or which one to offer the job to. Throughout the process some of the interviewers can develop a favorite candidate that they want to see hired. Interviewers will become advocates of hiring candidates they believe will make the best employees. This is often not a universal opinion, and the direct manager will usually make the final decision, but you can see how the candidates who create multiple advocates will have a higher probability of getting the job offer.

You can create advocates in your interview process by preparing well for each interview, regardless of who it is with. After preparing for the interview, you will need to get into a relaxed, professional, but likable frame of mind because the interviewers are also trying to imagine what it would be like to work with you.

This is how your answers are analyzed.

As a candidate, every answer you give in an interview must meet the minimum credibility standard. For example, taking credit for territory rankings or success in a sales position after working it for just three months is not credible if the typical sales cycle is nine to twelve months long for that industry.

Similarly, claiming to be downsized when your former company is hiring and expanding will also harm your credibility. If your answers seem credible then we can take a closer look at how strong those answers are.

Interviewers prioritize the strength of a candidate's answers when evaluating feedback and making hiring decisions. A strong answer instills the interviewer with confidence that you could be a good employee and directly influences the overall favorable impression that you leave upon them.

The hierarchy of answer impressiveness may vary depending on the type of interview questions and the industry or sector of the job. When you are organizing your memories in preparation for your interview, pay special attention to where your answers fall on this scale of impressiveness.

Hierarchy of impressiveness for interview answers.

1. Verifiable accomplishments (i.e., awards, recognition, publications, or rankings.).
2. Accomplishments, but they are harder to verify.

3. Good success stories that directly relate to the job.
4. A good example of past success that indirectly relates to the job.
5. An example that demonstrates a personality trait that fits the profile.
6. Demonstrating personality traits during interviews.
7. Hypothetical answers describing what you would do in a future situation.
8. Showing related work experience (Higher rank the more successful that experience was.).
9. Opinion: Self-descriptive statements trying to convince the interviewer how great you are.
10. Answering with a lot of words but avoiding the actual question that was asked.
11. Awkward silence.
12. Lying.

Companies do not have a formal hierarchy list that they follow, but interviewers do typically rank a candidates' answers based on this type of analysis. If you are interviewing for a job with a company in a commercial industry, then the strongest answers typically demonstrate how you made and/or saved your previous employers money. Use this hierarchy of impressiveness to focus on the strongest points that you should convey but stay away from memorizing verbatim answers.

Understand more by doing your own evaluation.

The interviewers come prepared to assess specific experiences and qualities, all while operating within the constraints of a limited time frame, which typically ranges from 30 to 60 minutes.

Let's continue the thought exercise by having you image that you have interviewed four different candidates with almost identical backgrounds.

Here is an overview of how well they interviewed with you:

1. Candidate directly highlighted experiences that match the skills we are looking for. Answers were concise and delivered confidently. When asked follow-up questions the candidate was able to provide more detail in a comfortable back and forth conversation. The candidate

asked insightful questions and expressed an interest in moving forward in the interview process.

2. Your questions were answered adequately. A couple of initial answers were too vague and required additional specific inquiries to gather the necessary information for assessing their suitability. You were able to gain an understanding of their skills, but not much about their personality or what they would be like to work with.
3. Responses were unfocused, vague, and tended to meander. The candidate provided long-winded explanations with irrelevant details. Time ran out, and by the end of the interview, you still lacked the essential information required to evaluate the candidate's suitability.
4. While you spoke about the company and job, the candidate made very little eye contact with you and was paying attention to other things. Before answering your questions, the candidate asked you to convince them that the role wasn't a step back in their career. When they spoke of their experience, they clearly believed that they were above the job.

If you were asked for your recommendation, which candidate(s) would you recommend moving forward in the interview process? Would you become an advocate for any candidate(s)? I hope you can begin to see the importance that preparing for interviews has on your ability to be successful compared to other candidates. Would your recommendations change if there were 2 candidates in each category for a total of 8?

Most interviewers categorize candidates into one of three groups: "Yes", "No", or "Maybe" based on their fit to the ideal profile. As the interview stages progress, we typically filter and refine the pool of candidates, so it becomes smaller with each stage. After interviewing an adequate number of candidates for the position, a decision is made regarding whether there are enough "Yes" candidates or if it's necessary to consider some of the "Maybe" candidates. Not all candidates who could do the job are moved forward, only the strongest candidates move to the next round of consideration.

All four of the hypothetical candidates from the thought exercise have the appropriate background for the job, but after their interviews only one or two of these would move forward. Every interviewer understands that the candidate they endorse will serve as a reflection of their competence as an interviewer, and the stronger that you interview the more confidence they have.

The candidate listed first out of the four would likely have most of the interviewers advocating for them. Candidate number two would likely have many interviewers recommending that they move forward in the process and are open to the idea that the candidate may interview stronger in the next round. The third candidate would likely have most interviewers recommending that they do not move forward in the process. While the fourth candidate would be a "No" for almost all who interviewed them.

Even though all four of these candidates could do the job, the first candidate will come across as a stronger match both in soft skills and in personality. No major red flags for the number two candidate, but they are less impressive than their competition. For the third candidate, they will almost always lose out to candidates like the first two. Candidate number four is very likely a problem employee waiting to happen.

How we assess candidate potential.

Most employers are looking for candidates who can grow and improve while doing an excellent job in their current role. To evaluate if a candidate has potential for this growth, most interviewers will assess certain traits. I have used the following list as my guidance in the past to determine candidate potential.

- *Motivation*

A fierce commitment to excel in the pursuit of unselfish goals. High-potential candidates have great ambition and want to leave their mark, but they also aspire to big, collective goals, show deep personal humility, and invest in improving everything they do.

- *Curiosity*

Candidates who possess a desire for personal growth tend to have a natural inclination towards exploring new experiences, seeking knowledge, and receiving honest feedback. These individuals remain open to learning and embracing change, recognizing that personal development is a continual process that requires dedication and an eagerness to expand their horizons.

- *Insight*

The capacity to gather and interpret data in a way that reveals fresh perspectives and opportunities is a valuable trait that sets candidates apart. Being able to discern patterns and connect seemingly unrelated information helps in identifying new possibilities and finding innovative solutions. This ability to gather and make sense of information is a critical skill for success in many industries.

- *Engagement*

Being able to communicate a compelling vision effectively is a highly sought-after skill by employers. Those who possess a talent for using both emotion and logic to persuade others are especially valuable. This skill can help build strong relationships, motivate teams, and drive the achievement of shared goals.

- *Determination*

The perseverance to pursue challenging objectives in the face of obstacles and the resilience to recover from setbacks. Hiring determined candidates can bring a sense of motivation and drive to the workplace, which can inspire others to work harder and achieve more. Determination is often an indicator of a candidate's passion for their work and their commitment to producing high-quality results. This quality can also help employers identify individuals who are likely to persevere through challenges and contribute to the company's success.

Understanding the perceptions that interviewers likely have.

Questions can also come from something that the interviewer reads on your resume or as a follow-up question prompted by one of your answers. You will be better prepared if you understand how others perceive your background, so that you can highlight your strengths and mitigate any shortcomings.

For instance, having a good record of accomplishment with a well-known and respected company is an advantage. However, most startups I have worked with in the past prefer a background that includes both a large established employer and some experience in a small company environment. The perception is that large organizations train their employees well and they can bring those best practices to their next job. Startups have a culture that is quite different from large organizations. The concern is that someone who is used to a big company environment might not understand enough about the entrepreneurial culture at a startup and leave after a short stay because it does not suit them.

I have interviewed candidates with strong academic backgrounds from prestigious institutions like Harvard, Stanford, Yale, Penn, Oxford, Duke, and others. I remember one candidate who had absolutely no industry experience, but projected arrogance during the interviews because of their education and did not move forward in the process. Having a strong academic background is a good thing, but it is far from the only thing that makes a candidate desirable. Your degrees and certifications demonstrate a minimum level of knowledge, in many cases they show that you are a hard worker, and if they are from exclusive institutions, it shows that you were admitted where most others were not. But, if you are not self-aware enough to realize that you do not know much about the industry yet, then you make a bad impression. Employees who think that they already know everything usually do not take responsibility for their mistakes, do not change what they are doing, and do not improve. It would have been far better for that candidate to have responded in ways that demonstrated that they understood there was much that they needed to learn but were eager to learn it. Academic success is simply an indication that they are capable of learning, not that they already know everything.

Candidates with a history of short-term employment will be viewed with suspicion, as it may suggest issues with skills or personality. During the interview process, it is crucial that we uncover any history of inferior performance or conflict with previous management/co-workers. Whatever your background is, it is important to think about how the interviewers are going to view it.

Getting some extra help – Understanding the recruiters.

You might work with a recruiter during your interview process, and they could be an outside/third-party or an inside/corporate recruiter. The term "Headhunter" refers to an outside recruiter who works with executive-level roles. Regardless of the type of recruiter you work with, there are some basic commonalities to their jobs, the most important being that if you impress them, they will often become your advocate.

Corporate Talent Acquisition Recruiters are given goals for the number of hires that they need to fill at their company. They are tracked on how long it takes them to fill the positions that they are assigned, a metric called "Time-to-Fill". In an increasing number of employers, the quality of the new employees ("Quality-of-Hire") is also tracked, things like retention, performance, and promotion of the employees hired by that recruiter reflect on his/her performance. Inside recruiters do not receive commission for filling an open position, but this is how their job performance and future promotions are evaluated. In most interview processes, after making the decision regarding your resume/application, these recruiters will conduct the initial phone screen. If you can impress the recruiter, they often turn into an advocate to get you hired so that they can close that opening and work on the other ten to forty openings they likely have.

Outside recruiters, including headhunters, have a direct financial incentive to become advocates for strong candidates. These are not employees of the company you are wishing to join, but vendors of that company. Most third-party recruiters are paid on a contingency basis, which means that the company does not pay them unless they hire a candidate from that recruiter. I want to be clear with you though, I do not even submit candidates to my clients if they are not a good fit because it will make me look bad. Sending a candidate who is a bad fit to a client leads that company to lose confidence in the recruiter and they will stop working with them. If you can impress an outside recruiter and they see a possible successful placement, then they will absolutely become an advocate for you.

Understanding the incentives that recruiters have will help you take advantage of their assistance. Outside recruiters have multiple client companies they work with so they can introduce you to opportunities at more than one employer if they are impressed by you. Inside recruiters have a deeper knowledge of the company that they work for, and the personalities of the people that you will be interviewing with. One or both will likely be involved in the final deliberations on who should receive the job offer. If impressed by you, both are likely to answer your questions and assist you throughout the interview process. Asking open-ended questions about what to expect or about the personalities of those who will be interviewing you is quite common, and you should utilize their help.

Not all recruiters are created equal of course, but if you find a good one that you trust and enjoy working with, it will benefit you to build a long-term professional relationship with them.

I once worked with a candidate who was a strong fit for the skills portion of the profile I was seeking. In fact, the candidate was overqualified for the position and what the company was willing to pay, but he still wanted to be interviewed for it. I made a good pitch to the hiring manager, but she felt that it just was not a good fit for what she wanted. After I explained this to the candidate, he did not want to accept that answer, so without informing me, he contacted the hiring manager directly. She not only told him the same answer that I had given, but she knew right away how inappropriate his actions were and told me that she now would never consider him for anything in the future.

This candidate was never going to get that job, but because of his hubris, he is not a candidate I will ever introduce to any hiring manager again. Be mindful of the relationships you have if you find a good recruiter.

How to Answer Behavioral-Based Interview Questions

Behavioral-based interview questions are based on the premise that past behavior is the best predictor of future behavior in similar situations. These questions are also known as competency-based, behavioral, situational-based, or performance-based interviews. There is a related style of questioning called skill-based interview questions. To succeed in these types of interviews, it's important to prepare in advance.

Situational-based interview questions are hypothetical questions and can be answered with a theory of what you would do, but the strongest answers demonstrate what you would do based on what you did in a comparable situation in the past. The following advice will work if you hear any of these terms. There is a simple exercise you can complete in preparation for these types of interviews that will significantly increase your success rate. Before I explain this in more detail, I want to cover the most common advice on how to answer these types of questions.

Behavioral interviews are designed to test your ability to work well in various scenarios, including high-pressure situations, tight deadlines, and urgent needs. The interviewer wants to see if your decisions and attitude match the profile of who they are hoping to hire.

In answering behavioral questions, you need to take the time prior to the interview to refresh your memory and think about which experiences you have had that relates most to each question before answering them. Preparing before the interview should help you be organized in your thoughts and be as confident as possible.

It is always best to answer these questions with a specific example, while also keeping your answers concise. Stick to the salient facts of the success story that you're telling. Give details related to the skills that you need to demonstrate without providing unnecessary and distracting information. The more details you give about how you have demonstrated the behaviors and skills that the interviewer is seeking, the less likely you will be asked follow-up questions.

There was a candidate I worked with that seemed to be a borderline yes or no fit for what we were looking for. I first interviewed several other candidates who looked better on paper, but they did not come across well in their interviews, so I decided to give this questionable candidate a chance. She was so well prepared with her answers to my behavioral questions that she stood out compared to all other candidates. Her answers were right on point to the qualities we were seeking, and she delivered them with detail and confidence. The hiring manager was not impressed by her resume either, but after interviewing her, the candidate sailed through the rest of the process and got the job. This candidate had obviously taken the time to organize strong examples that demonstrated exactly what we were looking for, and you should do the same if you want to interview successfully.

What is standard advice on how to respond to behavioral-based interview questions?

Here is a list of what you can do to prepare for behavioral interview questions:

1. Examples should be tailored to the perfect candidate.
2. Make a list of your previous efforts and significant achievements.
3. Formulate your answers using the S.T.A.R. technique, which I will explain in this chapter.
4. Be succinct and precise in your answers.

Examples should be tailored to the perfect candidate.

During a behavioral interview, it's important to remember that the interviewer is looking for specific qualities in a candidate. When responding to questions during a behavioral interview, tailor your responses to what the hiring manager is looking for in a candidate. For example, if the job description specifies that the business is seeking someone with three years of experience and a strong understanding of specific software programs, they will want to ask you about situations where you used these programs or something that is similar.

Make a list of your previous significant achievements.

Make a list of successes from your career that are relevant to the job you're applying for, and if you're early in your professional life, don't hesitate to use examples from your academic career if they're applicable. Your responses to these questions should conclude with how your actions resulted in success. If your company's sales have risen due to your work, explain how you got there and what you may do to achieve consistent outcomes in the future.

Formulate your answers using the S.T.A.R. technique.

The S.T.A.R. technique (Situation, Task, Action, and Result) is the most popular method for answering behavioral interview questions in a clear and thorough way. Some people may refer to it as S.O.A.R. (Situation, Obstacle, Action, and Result), but it's essentially the same thing. By using this technique, you can break down your responses into easy-to-follow components that effectively convey your experience. Each element of S.T.A.R. offers a framework for telling your story when answering these types of interview questions. With this technique, you'll be well-prepared to respond to questions in a way that showcases your skills and achievements and increases your probability of landing the job.

Here is an explanation of each stage and an example:

- **Situation**

Describe a situation relevant to the question asked that you have faced in your past, and any essential facts the interviewer should be aware of. If you are just beginning your career, it's fine to use situations from other experiences such as academia or sports. Prioritize pertinent information that relates to the position you are looking for.

Consider the following example of a situation: *"In my previous nursing role, we faced a critical shortage of staff during a flu outbreak, which significantly increased patient load and urgency."*

- **Task**

Tell the interviewer about the responsibilities that you had in this scenario. This explains the specifics of what you needed to accomplish on behalf of your former company to reach a goal.

As I will explain later in the chapter, this is the least important part of the S.T.A.R. technique.

Consider the following example of a task: *"My task was to manage patient care for an entire ward, ensuring all patients received timely treatment and care during this high-pressure period."*

- **Action**

Explain the steps that you took to meet your deadline and accomplish the objective you set for yourself. Create a list of the top talents that you want to convey to the interviewer for this stage, which should emphasize the skill you are attempting to demonstrate to the interviewer.

Consider the following example of an action: *"I prioritized critical cases, delegated tasks effectively among the available staff, and arranged for additional resources from other departments."*

- **Result**

Define the results achieved due to your actions. When feasible, provide statistics or specific quantifiable outcomes and how they impacted the business at the time. You want to give a clear timeline, completion timeline, and the impact of your decisions.

Consider the following example of a result: *"As a result of these efforts, we successfully managed the patient influx without compromising on care quality. Patient satisfaction scores during this period remained high, and the team morale was boosted by our collective efficiency."*

Be succinct and precise in your answers.

Make your answers as brief as possible, keeping them under two minutes. Preparing with a mentor or friend is an effective approach to keep your replies brief while directly addressing the substance of their questions. You can also give your answers to your own voicemail and listen back to them to check the length and quality of your answers. Keep in mind that the interviewer may shift gears and ask different follow-up questions, so be prepared to adapt accordingly. By preparing in advance and delivering concise, relevant responses, you'll make a strong impression and increase your success.

Examples of Behavioral-based interview questions:

1. Describe the most challenging situation you have had to deal with in the last year.
2. Describe a moment when you exceeded your manager's expectations to help a customer.
3. Tell us about a time when a colleague needed motivation and what you did to help them.
4. Tell us about a time when your workload was a problem. What steps did you take to address this problem?
5. Have you ever felt pressured to meet a deadline? What methods did you use to deal with this problem?
6. Describe a time when you committed a blunder that had a negative impact on your team. How did you deal with that situation?
7. Tell me about a time that you had to rapidly pick up a new skill. What was the outcome, and how did you go about learning your new skill?
8. Tell me about when you had to pitch an idea to upper management. What was the outcome?
9. Have you ever had a disagreement with a coworker about the project's direction? What did you do to come to a compromise with your coworker?

Using the S.T.A.R. method.

Describe the most challenging situation you have had to deal with in the past year.

"In the past year, I encountered a complex research issue that required a quick resolution to maintain the integrity of our study. One of the critical aspects was navigating a technical issue related to data analysis software, crucial for our ongoing research.

After identifying the issue, I immediately initiated a thorough investigation, collaborating with our research team to pinpoint the root cause. Recognizing the urgency, I proactively communicated the situation to my supervisor, outlining the potential impact on our research timeline. I worked closely with our IT specialists to rectify the technical glitch swiftly.

In the end, our collaborative efforts not only resolved the technical issue quickly but also ensured minimal disruption to our research timeline."

This answer is successful because it takes the interviewer through a success story where you are the star of that story, and your company benefited by having you as their employee. It mostly follows the S.T.A.R. method but illustrates why I am telling you that there is a more effective, and efficient method to prepare for a behavioral-based interview.

The best way to prepare.

1. Start with one or more blank sheets of paper and turn them horizontally to be in a landscape layout. (Of course, you can do this digitally if you prefer.)
2. Draw two vertical lines down the page so that you create three equal columns.
3. At the top of the left column write "Situation", center column "Action", and on the right "Results".
4. Re-read the optimal profile you wrote or the job advertisement, the duties, requirements, and any other parts that describe what the company is looking for in the person that they hire.
5. Using only bullet points, start listing specific examples from your career that relate to the ideal profile.

6. After you have put as many relevant examples as you can recall, set this page aside and when you remember another fitting example, come back to it, and jot it down. (This might take a couple of days.)
7. Once you have all the most relevant examples, re-write these bullet points, and rank them so that your best examples are listed at the top (the ones that you don't want to leave the interview without making sure you mention them.), and then list the remainder in descending order of impressiveness as they relate to the profile.

You will notice that I have removed the "T" from the S.T.A.R. technique. This is not because the tasks/responsibilities you had were unimportant, it's just that they are the least important compared to the situation, the action, and the results from your story. The benefit of removing the task is that you are more likely to remember a greater number of examples and their details if you use the S.A.R. (Situation, Action, Results) technique versus the S.T.A.R. technique. Some will advise you to use Situation *or* Task in the beginning of your answer, but I still feel that you will be more productive if we keep it as simple as possible.

Behavioral-based interviews can be exceedingly difficult if you do not prepare ahead of time. Using this S.A.R. exercise prior to your interview will help you recall examples and deliver a confident, successful answer. Confidence comes from being asked a question in an interview and taking a second or two to recall your list of examples, choosing the one that best fits that question, and delivering your success story. Without this preparation, I have seen many candidates freeze as they struggle to recall an example from their past. This comes across as less confident, less impressive, and sometimes less believable. You can find this S.A.R. exercise along with others in the ***COMPANION WORKBOOK The Ultimate Guide to Successful Job Interviewing.***

Final behavioral-based interview insights.

Over the years I have heard many candidates explain how they dislike behavioral-based interview questions because they believe that people can simply make up stories to get hired. These types of questions are just one tool used to make hiring decisions. Even though some candidates may believe that they are inventing the wheel for the first time, experienced recruiters and hiring managers can spot inconsistencies and check on claims made in answers. Candidates who are dishonest simply save the interviewer time by demonstrating why they should not be hired.

The most common mistake candidates make when answering behavioral-based interview questions is to avoid answering them altogether. For example, if a candidate is asked for an example and responds with a vague non-answer like "I deal with that all the time..." or "I have many clients who do that...", they have failed to provide a specific example related to the question. After a few vague answers, most interviewers will eliminate the candidate from consideration. This type of candidate comes across as someone who cannot follow simple directions or does not have good examples to use because they do not match what we are looking for.

Another mistake is not listening to the entire question. Candidates sometimes start to think about the example they want to use and stop listening to the interviewer. There is often part two or even three to the question and you need to juggle the skill of listening to everything that is being asked, while also searching your memory for the appropriate answer to use.

To prepare for behavioral-based interview questions, write out bullet points for success stories and practice saying them aloud. Avoid memorizing verbatim answers and instead speak naturally during the interview. Remember that interview questions are chosen to determine if a candidate fits the desired profile for the job. Answers should include examples of skills, temperament, experience, and talent that match what the company is looking for.

You should stay far away from canned, memorized verbatim answers as they will come across as very disingenuous. Stick to memorizing the bullet points of your examples and speaking naturally when answering these questions during the interview. Remember that the interviewer is also there to assess your personality fit, if you come across as someone being fake because you are reciting an answer, then you will be less successful.

Quick reference summary:

1. Prepare ahead of time using the S.A.R. exercise.
2. Relate all your examples to the ideal profile.
3. Practice saying your examples aloud before the interview.
4. Listen to the entire question.
5. Give real examples from your experience.
6. Focus on the main points that you need to make.
7. Do not make up examples.

How to Answer the Most Common Tough Interview Questions

Many job applicants have experienced the sinking feeling of being caught off-guard by unexpected or tough interview questions. While it is hard to predict exactly what a potential employer will ask, understanding common tough questions, their purpose, and how best to address them helps job seekers feel more confident and better prepared for their interviews.

Organizations ask interview questions to learn more about you and how much of a match you are to the perfect candidate they are seeking to hire. For example, the classic "tell me about yourself" question has stumped many candidates. While this seems simple, I have seen two types of candidates fail badly in answering this question: the overconfident and the intimidated. I will address these mistakes a little later in this chapter.

Successful candidates usually have prepared for common tough interview questions in advance, taking the time to tailor their answers to that specific organization or employer. This can make interviews go more smoothly and make applicants more impressive to interviewers. Some of the tough questions are a way to push applicants to think critically and creatively about their answers. Others are difficult because they catch candidates off guard.

No matter how challenging an interview may seem, getting hired depends largely on how prepared a candidate is relative to other applicants. Doing your best will depend on your ability to convey how you are a match to what they believe will make a successful employee. Your answers should be concise and relevant, connecting your experiences to the ideal profile.

Your thorough understanding of the job and the profile that the employer seeks will give you insights into the questions you will likely be asked while interviewing for that position. The most successful interview preparation usually includes answering these questions with your significant other or recording and listening to your answers before the interview.

Practice, practice, and practice again until you are comfortable and confident. Do not memorize answers verbatim, instead simply get comfortable with the main points that you need to make within each answer and then speak naturally.

I have interviewed thousands of job candidates that seem like a perfect fit on paper, but in the interview, they were less impressive than candidates who seemed to be not as strong of a fit based on their resume. To help you succeed, take a closer look at some of the most common difficult interview questions, and examples of how to answer them.

Difficult to answer questions and how to respond to them.

"Tell me about yourself."

Reason we ask: The interviewer is trying to evaluate how much of a match you are to what they want to hire. This question/statement is a quick way for us to gather certain information; do you understand the job and what we are looking for? Do you have the education and/or experience we want? For some jobs, we are evaluating your presentation skills.

Insights: This is a terrific opportunity to explain to the interviewer how you match what they are seeking. Answering such an open-ended question can lead many candidates to provide a long-winded, meandering answer with too much detail that is unrelated to the job. It is easier for the interviewer to follow your answer if you walk through your background in a chronological order, starting with school or when you entered your industry up until the present day. Good answers are concise, they include highlights of achievements that are relevant to the job and are typically between thirty and sixty seconds in length.

It can be tempting to choose a vague word like "Unique" or an all-purpose, safe option like "Hardworking," but such responses are generic and do not reveal anything to potential employers. Instead, highlight specific areas where your background matches the job requirements, such as your education, experience with specific software programs or languages, or other skills that are relevant to the position. If you can, try to connect a personal trait to the company culture or the job description.

To make your answer stand out, add a brief statement that sets you apart from other candidates. Specifically, you should include your Unique Value Proposition (U.V.P.). Your U.V.P. should be a brief statement that clearly explains your skills, experience, and unique strengths in a way that appeals to this employer. Based on your research or knowledge about the company or industry, mention something about yourself that makes you more qualified for the job than most other candidates. While it is easier for the interviewer to follow an answer in chronological order, starting your answer with a strong U.V.P. that demonstrates a solid match for the job is often the most impressive answer. To learn more about the U.V.P., please read my book ***SoaringME The Ultimate Guide to Successful Job Searching***.

What to avoid: As I mentioned earlier in this chapter, I have seen two types of candidates routinely fail when it comes to answering the questions, "Tell me about yourself", or "Why are you a good fit for this position?". The first type is the overconfident candidate who tends to use clichés and self-promoting language without providing any evidence to back up their claims. I once had a candidate repeatedly describe themselves as an "All-star" during an interview without offering anything that supported this statement. It was not convincing, and it made him look very underwhelming compared to good candidates. He did not move forward in the interview process.

The second type of candidate who often struggles with this question is the intimidated candidate. They may not see how their skills and experiences align with the position and fail to mention them in their answer. However, it is crucial to research the job and company beforehand and identify the ways in which you are a good match. Your answer should not be about bragging but about demonstrating your qualifications for the position.

Confidence is key when answering this question. Be sure to highlight your relevant experiences and skills that make you a strong fit for the position. Avoid using generic language and provide concrete examples to support your claims. Remember, it is not just about showcasing your skills and experiences, but also about demonstrating how they align with the job requirements and company culture. By preparing and delivering a strong answer, you can stand out as a top candidate for the job.

"What is your biggest weakness?"

Reason we ask: Your answer to this question should tell us how self-aware you are, and if you have a weakness that makes you not compatible with the job or company.

Insights: This is the same answer you would give if you were asked *"What is something your boss has told you that you need to work on?"*, or *"What is one thing that you would change about yourself?"*. Sincerity is especially important in this answer. Presenting a positive trait as a flaw of yours is an old trick that we see through, and it is not impressive. You should also try to stay away from a personality trait because those answers are full of pitfalls. Instead, discuss an actual professional shortcoming that you have identified, worked on, improved upon, and that will not negatively impact your performance in the job you are interviewing for. This demonstrates self-awareness and a commitment to professional growth.

Example answer of a candidate interviewing for a Nurse Midwife role: *"In my previous role as a Surgical Nurse, I realized that I sometimes struggled with the emotional aspect of patient care. Particularly in high-stress surgical situations, I found it challenging to* *maintain the level of emotional support that patients needed. To address this, I enrolled in workshops focused on enhancing empathy and communication skills. While the surgical setting demanded a different emotional response, I acknowledged my weakness and worked on building a more compassionate approach. Transitioning to a Nurse Midwife role, where emotional support is integral to the birthing process, aligns better with my commitment to providing comprehensive and empathetic care."*

The emotional skills needed to be a Surgical Nurse are not required to be an exceptionally good Nurse Midwife. The answer displays self-awareness and the ability to improve but does not make the interviewer doubt that the candidate is a match for the role.

What to avoid: It is crucial to avoid certain responses when asked about your biggest weakness in a job interview. The worst answer would be to claim that you do not have any weaknesses. This response portrays a lack of self-awareness and raises a red flag that you might be a difficult employee. The second-worst answer is to mention a skill from the optimal profile for the job, which would likely be perceived as not being the best candidate to hire. Cliché responses like "I'm a workaholic" or "I can be too driven by my work" come across as insincere and should be avoided. It's important to choose an actual professional weakness that you have identified, improved, and are continuing to work on.

"Why should I hire you over somebody else?"

Reason we ask: This answer will tell the interviewer how well you understand the job, how much of a match you are to what we want to hire, and some insight into your enthusiasm.

Insights: The best way to prepare for this question is by preparing for the *"Tell me about yourself."*, and *"What is your greatest strength?"* questions. Successful answers will show an understanding of the job and the profile that we are looking to hire. Provide a concise overview of how your experience and skills align with the position, including your U.V.P. Show why you are the best candidate for the job and the company without comparing yourself to others. Create a compelling and succinct explanation of why your services are valuable to the business.

Example answer for a candidate interviewing for a Certified Nursing Assistant job: *"I believe my background and qualities line up well with the requirements of this Certified Nursing Assistant position. My hands-on experience in patient care, strong understanding of medical procedures, and commitment to compassionate healthcare make me a suitable candidate. Beyond the technical skills, I bring a genuine passion for providing empathetic and personalized care to patients. I am not only seeking a job but an opportunity to contribute my skills and dedication to enhancing the well-being of those under my care. I am confident that my combination of practical experience, empathy, and enthusiasm sets me apart as the right fit for this role."*

What to avoid: Far too many candidates deliver a canned memorization verbatim answer to this question, and it comes off as insincere. It's best to avoid discussing other candidates or being negative about them, as it may indicate that you have difficulties working with others.

"Why are you interested in this job?"

Reason we ask: The answer to this question gives the interviewer insights into your career goals; how much you know about this position and company, whether you did your research, what your motivation is, how strong your motivation is, what is most important to you. All of those help us determine how much of a fit you are. Applicants who simply want any job become employees that do not stay long, and this question is an attempt to screen them out of the process.

Insights: Your response to this question should show that you have taken the time to research the company and the position, and that you are enthusiastic about the opportunity. While it is important to connect your background to the ideal candidate, the focus of your answer should be on the company itself. Identify two or three unique attributes of the company's culture, history, products, or reputation that differentiate it from other employers. Your response should demonstrate that you are motivated, professional, and have a genuine interest in the company and the position.

Example answer for a candidate interviewing for a Licensed Practical Nurse (LPN) job: *"I am very drawn to the LPN position at XYZ Medical Center because of your commitment to patient care and reputation for providing top-notch medical services. My career as a Licensed Practical Nurse has demonstrated my dedication to delivering compassionate care and ensuring the well-being of patients. I am particularly excited about the comprehensive healthcare services your facility offers and the opportunity to contribute my skills to a team focused on promoting health and recovery. Joining XYZ Medical Center aligns perfectly with my professional values and goals, and I am eager to contribute to your team and the standard of care that your institution is known for."*

What to avoid: Mentioning compensation or benefits and displaying a lack of enthusiasm in your tone or body language are mistakes to avoid when answering this question. Focusing too much on salary and perks can give the impression that you are not passionate about the job or the company, but only interested in what you can get out of it. Similarly, a disinterested tone or negative body language can give the impression that you are not fully invested in the opportunity, which can be a turn-off for the interviewer.

"What is your biggest achievement?"

Reason we ask: The answer to this question should give the interviewer insight into both your skills and your personality. When you choose what you consider to be your biggest achievement, it tells us what you consider to be most important. Understanding what your priorities are in the workplace will help us determine if you are a good fit for our company culture. We also need a certain level of skill in the people that we hire, so understanding what you did and how well you did it for your biggest achievement will inform us about your skill level.

Insights: Many people struggle with answering this question because they are not used to promoting themselves. However, it is a vital opportunity to showcase your accomplishments and how they align with the job you are interviewing for. This is a chance to demonstrate not just an accomplishment, but also the kind of effect you are likely to have, such as being a good co-worker or increasing the company's profit. Depending upon the ideal fit for this job, you may highlight professional or personal achievements if they demonstrate that you are a good match. Practicing your answer beforehand can help you feel more at ease with selling yourself during the interview.

Example: A hospital is hiring a Registered Nurse and critical thinking is a must have trait. They would prefer previous experience, but it is not required.

Answer 1: *"One of my most significant achievements as a Registered Nurse was during an emergency situation at ABC Hospital. A critically ill patient was admitted with a range of symptoms that didn't immediately align with a clear diagnosis. Drawing on my experience, I led a rapid assessment, coordinated with specialists, and facilitated a collaborative diagnostic process. Through careful critical thinking and decisive action, we identified a rare but treatable condition, enabling prompt intervention and ultimately saving the patient's life."*

Answer 2: *"As a recent nursing graduate, my most notable achievement lies in successfully applying critical thinking skills during my clinical rotations. One challenging scenario was where a patient exhibited unexpected symptoms, I collaborated with my preceptor and the healthcare team to conduct a thorough assessment. By analyzing the data, considering various possibilities, and seeking guidance when needed, we identified an underlying issue that required immediate attention. This experience showcased my ability to apply critical thinking in real-world situations and reinforced the importance of* *continuous learning in the nursing profession. I am excited to bring this skill set to your healthcare team and further develop as a Registered Nurse at your esteemed institution."*

What to avoid: Do not give a vague response, instead use a specific achievement. It's essential to be honest and avoid taking undue credit for something that was not solely your accomplishment. If you were part of a team, make sure to explain your significant contribution to the success. This answer should be backed by specific examples and not be merely a general statement. Be prepared for follow-up questions that may scrutinize your individual role in the achievement.

"What would your co-workers say about you?"

Reason we ask: Being self-aware is a particularly important soft skill for many organizations. Understanding how your behavior is perceived by others allows you to get along better with co-workers and thus make the team more productive. Your answer to this question should give us an idea of how self-aware you are, and about your personality. We will compare your answer to all other evidence we have or observe about you. We want to see if you would be a good fit for the company culture and this question also helps us make that determination.

Insights: Prepare ahead of time for this question by going through an honest assessment of your own strengths, then compare those to the ideal fit of what the company is looking for. Make yourself a list of anecdotes from your work that demonstrate the skills that this employer is looking for. When answering this question, highlight one or at most two of your strengths that align with the job requirements. Start by telling the interviewer about these strengths and then back them up with examples from your past.

Example answer: *"In my current role as an Advanced Practice Registered Nurse, my co-workers would likely describe me as a collaborative and compassionate team member. I consistently strive to foster a positive and cooperative work environment, actively participating in interdisciplinary teams to ensure comprehensive patient care. An example of this collaborative approach was during a recent case where I worked closely with nurses, physicians, and other healthcare professionals to develop and implement a tailored care plan."*

This answer demonstrates both that the candidate provides high quality patient care, but also that he/she works well within a team.

What to avoid: Do not make up skills that you don't have, or examples that did not happen. We do check some of your answers and compare notes with others who interview you during the process. **Being dishonest is the fastest and most sure-fire way to guarantee that you don't get the job.**

"What are your biggest strengths?"

Reason why we ask: This is a straightforward way for us to assess what you are best at and if that matches what we wish to hire. Your answer may also give us further insight into your personality, such as determining if you are self-aware and our view of a good fit.

Insights: This is about demonstrating the value of your labor to this employer. The difficult aspect is ensuring that the correct qualities are emphasized. When applying for an accounting job, for example, answering with "creative thinking" as your biggest strength would be a failure. Instead, highlight a skill that is more applicable to the accounting job, such as "attention to detail", or "organizational skills.".

Always keep in mind that there are other applicants competing with you for the job. It is advantageous to highlight a skill that sets you apart from other applicants, or that you excel in.

Notable strengths do not necessarily have to be hard skills; some employers are looking for the right personality that can be trained. Therefore, behavioral qualities such as tenacity or resilience might be essential when analyzing the ideal profile for the job.

After explaining what you believe to be your greatest strength that applies to this role, you need to provide evidence that this is a strength of yours. You should give an example of a time when you displayed this strength and how it produced a positive result. A strong example that demonstrates your skill is critical to your answer being more successful than other candidates. The final part of your answer should circle back to the job that you are interviewing for. Simply add a brief statement at the end of your answer to explain how this strength will make you more successful in this position.

Follow these steps to prepare for this question:

1. Make a list of your biggest strengths, experience, education, training, hard and soft skills.
2. Self-assess and rank the skills on your list in the order in which they are your strongest attributes.
3. Make a list of the desired qualities for the job, based on your understanding of the ideal profile.
4. Start with the first listed attribute that the company desires, and if it is listed as one of your top strengths, this should be the focus of your answer. If not, go to the second listed attribute on the company list. Continue until you find a genuine strength of yours that is highest on both lists.

If you cannot find an overlap from both lists, but you feel like one of your strengths will make you successful in this role, you need to tailor your answer to spend a little more time persuading the interviewer how this skill relates to the job. It is fine if you have two strengths that you can highlight, just keep your answer under two minutes long.

Example answer: *"My dedication to precision and vigilant monitoring in anesthesia administration was evident in a recent complex surgery. The surgery involved a patient with a pre-existing medical condition that posed unique challenges. As the procedure unfolded, I meticulously monitored the patient's vital signs and anesthesia levels, recognizing subtle changes that could have escalated into a critical situation. Midway through the surgery, unexpected complications arose, requiring immediate intervention. The patient's response to anesthesia began to deviate from the anticipated norm, and my astute monitoring allowed me to detect this deviation promptly. With a swift and precise adjustment to the anesthesia dosage, I was able to stabilize the patient's vital signs and ensure the safe progression of the surgery. I believe that this experience underscores my suitability for the Nurse Anesthetist role, emphasizing adaptability and unwavering attention to detail in critical situations."*

The impression this answer gives is that not only is this candidate organized, has good attention to details but also able to handle the pressures of the job.

What to avoid: The way you answer this question can reveal a lot about your character and suitability for the job.

Overconfidence may suggest that you are not open to constructive criticism and unwilling to improve. Conversely, being too modest may lead the interviewer to question your self-assurance and ability to excel in the role. The key is to strike a balance between confidence and humility, demonstrating that you are self-aware and coachable. Choose a strength that is specific and relevant to the job, avoiding generic or overly common answers.

"Why are you leaving your current job?" / "Why did you leave your previous job?"

Reason we ask: The answer to this question informs us about your motivation, and whether this career move makes enough sense to lead us to believe that you will be a long-term employee for us. The tricky part of this question is how much we can learn about your personality.

Insights: Even if the complaints are genuine, potential hires are not seen favorably when they complain about their current/previous employer, colleagues, or bosses. Instead, you should be honest but focus on what you want to go towards and not about what you are leaving. Match your desires for what it is that you want out of your next career step with the things that you would get from this new job. Always try to find a way to relate it back to how you are a good fit for this new opportunity.

Your answer might be different depending upon how you left your previous employment, so I am providing multiple scenarios and example answers.

Example answer for someone who voluntarily left/are leaving on good terms with their employer.

"I am grateful for the opportunity that I had at ABC Clinic, it was a wonderful experience but it's just time for me to take on a new challenge and show that I can accomplish even more than I already have. Your clinic will provide me with the opportunity to do that."

Example answer for someone who voluntarily left/are leaving on less than good terms with their employer.

"I learned a lot in my time with ABC Medical Center, but over time I realized what I really need is an opportunity that is going to both challenge me and allow me to care for patients that I can be enthusiastic about. I really like what I have learned about your facility

and medical care. This is a better fit for me and where I want to take my career."

Example answer for someone who was laid-off.

"Unfortunately, my employer went through a re-structuring in April. Since I was one of the most recent hires, I was part of a group that was let go. I have received an above average performance review, and my manager will be one of my references. The work that I had done well in that position is very similar to your position so I'm confident I will get up to speed very quickly."

Example answer for someone who was terminated.

"When I was initially hired it was because they were looking to bring a different skill set into ABC Clinic. I made appropriate changes, and we did increase patient satisfaction scores by 33%, but it quickly became clear that the head of my department and I have different styles. I learned that to thrive, I need an innovative and collaborative environment, which is exactly what I see in your clinic."

Notice that this answer is not negative towards the previous employer or boss, makes the point that at least some of the work done was good, and brings it all back to being a good fit for this new job. It does not give every detail about being fired and does not tell a lie. You should expect follow-up questions about some of the details, but continue to be concise, honest, positive, and professional. If you made a mistake at your previous job, explain how you have learned from it and why it will not be a problem for your next employer.

What to avoid: Airing out your grievances or dirty laundry from any of your past employers. Going into too much detail about your reasons, or even getting emotional as you think about the circumstances. Do not lie about how you left, if they offer you the job the company will check your background. Even if you get hired and they find out later that you lied, most companies will terminate you immediately.

"What are your salary expectations?"

(See the later chapter entitled *The Job Offer*.)

Common Interview Questions for Nursing Jobs

These are common interview questions that you may face as you progress in your career.

"Describe a challenging situation you faced during your clinical rotations and how you handled it."

Reason we ask: Your response to this question helps us assess if you possess the necessary personality traits and skills, such as empathy, adaptability, and the ability to handle pressure.

Example answer: *"During my clinical rotations, I encountered a challenging situation in the pediatric ward. There was a sudden surge of patients with varying needs, and it required swift prioritization. I took the lead in organizing the workflow, ensuring critical cases received immediate attention while supporting my colleagues. This* *experience reinforced my passion for nursing, emphasizing the importance of teamwork, adaptability, and providing compassionate care under pressure."*

This answer demonstrates a genuine commitment to nursing, an ability to handle challenges, and a collaborative approach to patient care.

What to avoid: Stay away from generic statements like *"I want to help people"* or *"I have a passion for healthcare,"* as we want a specific example, and your answer will lack impact without it. Avoid giving the impression that you are solely interested in the job for personal benefits or to escape your current situation. Focus on specific aspects of the nursing profession that inspire you and give an example that highlights how your unique qualities align with the demands of the job.

"Please give us examples of your experience in basic patient care."

Reason we ask: Your response to this question helps us gauge your practical experience in fundamental patient care tasks. It allows us to assess your hands-on skills, attention to detail, and understanding of nursing basics.

Example Answer: *"Throughout my clinical rotations, I worked on basic patient care. One notable example is when I assisted in the daily activities of elderly patients, ensuring they maintained proper hygiene, assisting with mobility, and providing emotional support. Additionally, I administered medications following the prescribed protocols, being precise and following safety measures. These experiences developed my ability to prioritize patient well-being and deliver compassionate care in both routine and critical situations."*

This response provides general instances of hands-on patient care, showcasing the candidate's practical skills and commitment to their nursing duties. The example was not a specific patient, but it was about specific tasks for a group of patients that demonstrated the skills needed for the job.

What to Avoid: Avoid overused phrases like *"I am detail-oriented"* without supporting them with specific instances. Do not embellish or provide inaccurate information about your experience. Instead, focus on real, demonstrable experiences that highlight your competence in basic patient care tasks.

"How do you ensure that patient records are accurate and complete, and what steps do you take to avoid documentation errors?"

Reason we ask: Your response to this question helps us assess your attention to detail, commitment to accuracy in patient care, and understanding of the importance of precise documentation in the nursing profession.

Example Answer: *"I prioritize having accurate and complete patient records. I use a systematic approach and double-check information during the documentation process. Making sure that all entries are timely, reflecting the most recent patient status. Regular audits and reviews of my documentation help promptly identify and rectify any potential errors. Moreover, I collaborate closely with other healthcare professionals to cross-verify information, fostering a team-based approach to accurate record-keeping. I am committed to precision in my documentation, it is part of my dedication to providing high-quality patient care."*

This response provides a detailed approach to ensuring accurate patient records, emphasizing the candidate's commitment to precision and collaboration.

What to Avoid: Don't use generic statements like *"I am careful with documentation"* without providing specific strategies. Avoid downplaying the significance of documentation in patient care. Focus on practical steps you take to ensure accuracy and avoid giving the impression that you neglect the importance of meticulous record-keeping in nursing.

"Share a specific example of a challenging patient assessment you've delt with. How did you navigate it, and what was the outcome."

Reason we ask: This question allows us to assess your clinical judgment, problem-solving skills, and ability to handle challenging healthcare situations. It gives us insight into your approach to patient care and your adaptability in critical moments.

Example Answer: *"During a night shift, I encountered a challenging assessment involving an elderly patient with multiple chronic conditions. The symptoms were complex, and the initial assessment revealed conflicting information. I used a thorough and systematic approach. I collaborated with the healthcare team to gather additional data, consulted with specialists, and ensured the patient received prompt diagnostic tests. Through these steps, we identified the underlying issues and adjusted the care plan accordingly. The outcome was a timely and accurate diagnosis, leading to improved management of the patient's health."*

This response provides a specific example of a challenging patient assessment, showcasing the candidate's collaboration, systematic approach, and positive outcome in patient care. The answer would be more impactful if it gave additional details about the conditions, symptoms, tests given, etc., but it does a good job of using a specific case to demonstrate skills, experience, and judgement.

What to Avoid: Vague answers that lack specific details or outcomes. Don't blame others or emphasize difficulties without highlighting your problem-solving strategies. Avoid downplaying the significance of the situation or providing incomplete information about the patient's assessment. Instead, provide a specific success story of a challenging scenario, your proactive approach, and the positive impact on patient care.

"Please share a situation where you identified a medication-related issue, and how did you address it to ensure the patient's well-being."

Reason we ask: This question helps us evaluate your attention to detail, critical thinking skills, and commitment to patient safety. It provides insight into your competence to identify and resolve medication-related challenges, a crucial aspect of nursing responsibilities.

Example Answer: *"During a medication administration round, I noticed a potential discrepancy in a patient's prescribed dosage. Upon thorough review, I identified a prescribing error that could have led to an adverse reaction. To address this, I immediately consulted the healthcare team, including the prescribing physician. We collaboratively discussed the issue, verified the correct dosage, and adjusted the medication plan accordingly. The outcome was that we averted harm to the patient, and it reinforced my commitment to* *accurate medication management for the well-being of those under my care."*

This response illustrates the candidate's attentiveness, collaboration skills, and dedication to ensuring patient safety in medication administration.

What to Avoid: You shouldn't downplay the significance of the medication-related issue or provide incomplete details about your actions. Stay away from blaming others without emphasizing your proactive steps. Avoid using vague language that doesn't clearly convey your role in resolving the situation. Focus on specific instances, your collaborative approach, and the positive impact on patient well-being.

"Share an example of a situation where you identified a deviation in vital signs during surgery and how you responded to ensure patient safety and well-being."

Reason we ask: This question allows us to assess your ability to recognize and address critical situations, and your commitment to patient safety. It provides insight into your decision-making process in high-stakes medical scenarios.

Example Answer: *"During a surgical procedure, I noticed a deviation in the patient's vital signs that raised my concerns. I alerted the surgical team and initiated a thorough assessment. We identified an unexpected bleeding complication that needed immediate attention. I coordinated with the team to control the bleeding, communicated effectively with the anesthesiologist to adjust medication levels, and continuously monitored the patient's vital signs. Our collaborative efforts stabilized the patient, ensuring a positive outcome."*

This answer highlights the candidate's clinical vigilance, quick decision-making, and collaborative skills in responding to a critical situation in surgery.

What to Avoid: Do not blame others without emphasizing your proactive steps. Avoid downplaying the significance of the situation or providing vague details about your actions. Additionally, don't overemphasize your personal achievements without acknowledging the collaborative efforts of the surgical team. Focus on specific instances, your coordinated response, and the positive impact on patient safety.

"Share an example of a high-stress situation you've encountered in your nursing career and how you effectively managed stress to maintain focus on patient care."

Reason we ask: This question helps us assess your skills in stress management, communication, critical thinking, empathy, and adaptability.

Example Answer: *"Last month in the emergency department, we faced an influx of critical patients during a sudden mass casualty event. The intensity was overwhelming, but my focus remained on delivering the best patient care possible. To manage the stress, I prioritized tasks, delegated responsibilities within the team, and maintained open communication. Despite the high-stress situation, our team coordinated seamlessly, and every patient received timely care. This is not an isolated occurrence, but it did reinforce to me the importance of teamwork, adaptability, and personal well-being in providing quality nursing care during demanding situations."*

This response demonstrates the candidate's ability to handle high-stress situations, prioritize patient care, and promote effective teamwork in a healthcare setting.

What to Avoid: Focus on specific instances, your stress management strategies, and the positive impact on patient care. Avoid downplaying the significance of the situation or providing vague details about your actions. Do not blame others without emphasizing your proactive steps. Additionally, don't overemphasize your personal achievements without acknowledging the collaborative efforts of the emergency team.

"Please discuss your experience and approach to providing postpartum care, including the assessments and support you offer to new mothers during the postpartum period."

Reason we ask: This question allows us to evaluate your expertise in postpartum nursing care, understanding of the unique challenges faced by new mothers, and your commitment to providing comprehensive support during this critical period.

Example Answer: *"My approach involves thorough assessments of physical and emotional aspects, paying close attention to signs of postpartum complications or mood disorders. I prioritize open communication, offering guidance on breastfeeding, infant care, and postpartum recovery. I create a supportive environment where new mothers feel heard and empowered. Collaborating with the healthcare team, I ensure a holistic approach to postpartum care, emphasizing the importance of mental health and fostering a positive transition into motherhood."*

This response illustrates the candidate's expertise, patient-focused care, and commitment to the well-being of new mothers during the postpartum period. The response would be even more impactful if it added a specific example that demonstrates these approaches.

What to Avoid: Do not overlook the emotional aspect of postpartum support. Avoid minimizing the importance of comprehensive assessments and collaboration with the healthcare team.

"How do you prioritize and allocate resources, including staffing levels to different units or shifts based on patient acuity and workload demands?"

Reason we ask: This question assesses your strategic thinking, organizational skills, and ability to make informed decisions in managing nursing resources. It reveals your understanding of patient acuity and workload dynamics, critical for effective nursing management.

Example Answer: *"I prioritize based on patient acuity, ensuring that high-need units receive adequate staffing levels. Regular assessments of workload demand guide my real-time adjustments to staffing, allowing for flexibility during peak periods. I collaborate closely with charge nurses and utilizing predictive tools, I proactively address potential imbalances."*

This response demonstrates the candidate's strategic approach, adaptability, and effective communication in resource allocation for nursing units. The response would be even more impactful if it added a specific example that demonstrates these approaches.

What to Avoid: Avoid rigid approaches that do not consider the dynamic nature of patient acuity and workload demands. Avoid generic statements without specific examples or strategies for resource allocation. Don't overlook the importance of ongoing assessments and collaboration with nursing staff. Focus on tangible instances, your leadership in resource management, and the positive impact on patient care.

Successfully Answer Technical Interview Questions

Technical interviews are meant to measure a candidate's skill level in an area that is required to be successful in the job. They are commonly used in tech, engineering, finance/accounting, medical, and other technical types of jobs. The questions will vary depending upon the specific technology used and they do tend to change from one interviewer to the next, so in this chapter I offer an overview of what to expect.

You can find online resources that provide up-to-date technical/medical questions that are asked at specific employers. Keep in mind that the interview processes at most companies are designed to screen for skills, but the specific questions asked are often left up to the individual interviewer. You will likely be asked variations of the questions found online so preparing for those will still lead to success. I suggest researching technical interview questions at the company you are applying to, and some of their competitors to prepare further. Start with a simple search online of the employer's name, followed by "medical interview questions", "interview", "interview questions", or "technical interview".

It is crucial that you have a solid understanding of the specific medical technology/treatment/procedure or skill they want to evaluate. By doing your research and practicing those skills, you can approach any technical interview with confidence and increase your probability of landing the job.

Expect technical nurse interview questions to evaluate these areas:

- **Clinical Scenario Questions.**
- **Skills Demonstration.**
- **Patient Assessment.**
- **Case Study Analysis.**
- **Equipment Familiarity.**
- **Medication Administration Questions.**
- **Pathophysiology and Pharmacology.**
- **Emergency Response.**

During a technical interview or the portion of your interview covering technical questions, it is not just your medical skills that are being evaluated. The interviewer is also looking to assess your personality and soft skills. If you are being considered for a collaborative position, communication is a critical skill that the interviewer will be evaluating. Solving a problem is one thing, but being able to communicate your thought process and ideas is also important. A successful employee will be someone who can work collaboratively with others to achieve a common goal. Thus, candidates who engage in a back-and-forth conversation with the interviewer while discussing their problem-solving process tend to be more successful in these interviews.

Also, intellectual curiosity and passion for medicine are far too overlooked in technical interviews. Companies are much more likely to hire a person with passion who can be coached-up on their hard skills, than an expert who lacks enthusiasm for their work.

Examples of technical interview behavioral-based questions.

"Tell me about a case you worked on that did not go well."

And *"Tell me about the most challenging diagnosis you have faced in the past couple of years. How did you solve it?"*

What are we looking for? That you can overcome challenges and work well within a team.

"Share insights into a healthcare-oriented project you've undertaken independently."

What are we looking for? Your passion.

"Describe an instance in your nursing experience when you were tasked with something unfamiliar."

What are we looking for? Ability to work independently, and your self-motivation.

Examples of technical interview direct questions.

"What online resources do you use to help you do your job?"

What are we looking for? Your passion, resourcefulness, and ingenuity.

"How do you keep your medical skills current?"

What are we looking for? Your passion and professionalism.

"Imagine you're not deeply familiar with healthcare technology; how would you describe the role of advanced technologies, like 'EHR systems,' in patient care?"

(EHR systems represent the technology used in this job or your past job.)

What are we looking for? Your ability to communicate complex technical concepts to non-technical individuals, displaying your proficiency in both technical knowledge and effective communication skills.

Suggestions to prepare for this part of the technical interview:

1. Study for technical interviews through current websites and online videos to learn the latest questions you are likely to be asked.
2. Study the medical technology used at the employer and the position.
3. Focus on refreshing your knowledge of clinical skills, making sure that you are up to date on nursing practices, and being ready to discuss experiences that demonstrate competence in various aspects of patient care.

If you are unfamiliar with the medical technology, illness, or treatment that you are being asked about, clarify the question, admit that you are not familiar with it, then talk about your knowledge of an adjacent technology, illness, or treatment. The point of studying for a technical interview is not necessarily to give the perfect correct answer to all problems, but more to demonstrate knowledge or a grasp of basic technical information, and a solid thought process. So, make sure that you can demonstrate a solid foundation of knowledge in the relevant areas. Avoid getting sidetracked by minor details and stay focused on the main issue at hand.

The Do's and Don'ts of Interviewing

There are a few key factors that can make or break your success in any interview process. To help you out, I've put together a list of these factors for you to review and keep in mind.

Things that you should do for more successful interviews.

Be fully prepared before your interview.

To succeed in the interview, you need to prepare yourself by doing thorough research. Start by gathering as much information as possible about the company, their mission, and how the position you are interviewing for will contribute to achieving their goals. Spend time learning all you can about the firm, its history, strategy, and executives. The more you know about the company, the more comfortable you will feel aligning yourself with their perfect candidate and the more insightful the questions that you ask will be. Pay particular attention to whatever you can discover about the individuals who will be interviewing you, maybe you have things in common, and learning about them will lead to questions you may want to ask during the interview.

To prepare for the specific job, study the job description, identify what qualities the ideal candidate should have, and think of ways to highlight your strengths that align with those qualities. If possible, do your preparation well in advance so that you are not cramming for this test up until the last minute. Your aim should be to relax for the six to twenty-four hours prior to your actual interview. I suggest spending part of the hour right before your interview listening to something that makes you happy and puts you in a positive mood. You want to be professional but also relaxed and enjoyable to speak with, as personality is a big part of the hiring decision.

Dress for the job you are interviewing for.

You should dress for the job that you want, in fact, a notch or two above the day-to-day attire for that job. We assume that the version we see in the interviews is you at your best. If you are interviewing for a job that will require you to dress business-casual and you interview wearing jeans and a T-shirt, that shows a lack of understanding, professionalism, and/or interest.

Express interest and enthusiasm for the opportunity.

One of the worst mistakes I have seen repeatedly made by candidates is when they are not sure if they genuinely want the position, and this lack of commitment shows in their demeanor during the interview. They come across poorly because they are seen as uninterested and get eliminated from the process. Ultimately, you want that decision to be yours to make. If you are offered the job and decide it is not the right career move, that's okay for you because it is your decision. However, if you come across as being unenthusiastic then the interviewer may decide that you are not their best choice for the job. Near the end of the interview, ask about the next steps, express what you like about the company and the opportunity.

Have good eye-contact and body language.

Showing a lack of presence during an interview indicates a lack of interest, enthusiasm, and professionalism. This type of behavior can hinder your chances of being hired, as employers prefer candidates who show genuine interest and enthusiasm. Employers try to stay away from hiring uninterested, indifferent, and unenthusiastic candidates because they tend to end up being short-term workers that do not provide high quality work.

Listen carefully to each question, and if needed clarify.

Being mentally present during an interview is crucial for a candidate to succeed. It's common to get lost in your own thoughts and focus on what you're going to say next, but failing to pay attention to the interviewer's question can result in a poor answer. To avoid this mistake, listen carefully to the question and then take a moment to gather your thoughts before answering. I might ask you a re-direct question to see if I can get you back on track, but many interviewers won't.

Practice before your interview.

Do not memorize your answers but practice delivering your main points to become more confident in your delivery. You can do this by calling your own voicemail and leaving your answers so that you can then listen to yourself. Alternatively, consider finding a friend or colleague to conduct "mock interviews" with you. When I taught interviewing in person, the most effective exercise that I used was to have the candidate play the role of the interviewer and ask questions based on the desired candidate profile to determine whether they would be a good fit. Through this process, you can gain valuable insights into areas you need to improve upon in your own answers.

Send a thank you email or note after every interview.

It is best to send a thank you within 24 hours after your interview, or if the interviewer tells you that they will be making their decision by a certain day, you can send it one day before that decision. In most industries, you should do this via email, but if the industry is high touch and personal in nature, then a physical note is better. If you do not have the email address for the interviewer, send it to the recruiter and ask them to forward it.

Thank you emails/notes should be short, typically 3-4 sentences long and should include:

1. Thank the interviewer for their time.
2. Remind them of the top 1 or 2 things about why you are a fit for the job that you believe impressed them.
3. If needed, try to mitigate any obvious concerns about your fitness for the job. (One sentence.)
4. Convey interest in moving forward with the interview process or receiving an offer for the job.

This is a process, and you will not get every job that you want.

Perseverance is key in the job interview process. Stay resilient and learn with every interview that you have. Even if you have a less than perfect interview, it is important to stay positive and learn from your mistakes. Take an honest assessment of your performance and make the small adjustments needed to improve your approach. It can be challenging, but keeping a positive attitude is essential for success.

Early in my career I worked with a recent college graduate that had no professional experience but who knew that she wanted to become a pharmaceutical sales representative. She was a little socially awkward, but likable and even though she was not a top-tier candidate, I wanted to help her. I had sent her out on interviews with two of my client companies and she did okay but did not receive a job offer from either. She was also interviewing on her own with other companies. Finally, she landed a job with a major pharmaceutical company and has since spent more than twenty years working in the career that she wanted. She got better at interviewing each time she did it, and it ultimately paid off. You must be persistent, remain positive, and as confident as possible for each interview that you go on.

Things that you should avoid for more successful interviews.

Arriving late.

For a face-to-face meeting you should arrive ten to fifteen minutes before the scheduled interview. However, for phone or video interviews, make sure to be ready three to five minutes before the scheduled time, whether it's logging into a video platform or having your phone nearby and fully charged. Also avoid being excessively early for your interviews.

No call/no show.

Failing to show up for your interview without any notice is one of the best ways to ensure that you're not going to be considered for the job. More than just the job for that interview, it is quite easy for something like this to follow you at some point in the future. A no call/no show makes such a bad impression that people will remember you in a negative way for a long time.

Sounding as though your answers are just rehearsed words that you think you are supposed to say.

Although it is important to prepare for expected interview questions, appearing too rehearsed will backfire against you. Focus on remembering the main points that you want to include in your answers, but do not be scripted. Practice ahead of time, but do not try to memorize your answers word-for-word. If you remember the main points and can be relaxed and sincere during the interview, you will do much better.

Speaking negatively about previous jobs.

When interviewing for a job, it's important to maintain a positive attitude and avoid speaking negatively about previous employers or colleagues. Speaking negatively can appear as gossipy and portray you as a probable future toxic ex-employee for this new company. Most interviewers are aware that there are two sides to every story so when they hear someone mention anything bad about a previous employer, they may believe that you were also part of the issue.

Focus on the positive aspects that you are going towards. Discuss the things you have done, the objectives you have met, and perhaps the connections you have formed. It is better to speak about a learning experience if you are questioned about a bad event. It is simply more attractive to hear that you are looking to move to a company like the one you are interviewing for, than to give the impression that you might be a problem employee if hired.

Delay responding to recruiters or hiring managers.

Recruiters will often ask for feedback after you interview with somebody besides themselves. Hiring managers and recruiters may also request clarification on something you mentioned during an interview. Failing to provide timely responses or withholding information gives the impression that you are not motivated to get the job.

Over-explaining.

When answering interview questions, it's important to be concise and to the point. Do not give long-winded meandering answers. Thirty to sixty second answers are ideal for most questions and tend to feel too long at about ninety seconds. Wait for follow-up questions to go into granular detail, but still try to be concise while also answering what you were asked.

Giving vague answers.

A vague answer is one that every candidate can provide such as *"That happens all the time"*. When answering interview questions, make sure to provide specific examples to support your responses. Vague answers can come across as evasive and can give the impression that you are trying to hide something or are not being truthful. Remember, the interviewer is trying to assess your skills and experience, so providing concrete examples helps to demonstrate your qualifications and build credibility. Avoid giving general or overly broad responses, and instead provide details that highlight your strengths and accomplishments. Be concise with your main points or example without over-explaining.

Demonstrating a lack of responsibility.

When discussing past mistakes, avoid blaming others. During an interview, you may be asked to talk about a time when you made a mistake at work. It's important to take ownership of your actions and avoid placing the blame solely on others.

Not getting the most out of your time.

Successful interviews are not only about answering questions, but they are also about you gathering information. If you only focus on answering questions and do not ask any, it can leave a negative impression on the interviewer. Prepare yourself by researching the business ahead of time and writing down the questions you want to ask. Use these to help guide you when using the Answer/Ask technique, or when it feels appropriate. Most interviewers will leave time at the end of the interview for you to ask questions, so be sure to take advantage of this opportunity. Asking good questions demonstrates your interest in the job and gaining information can give you an advantage over other candidates.

Giving a bad impression of your personality.

When interviewing for a job, be aware that certain personality traits may lead the interviewer to screen you out of the hiring process. They typically don't go into an interview with this list and test you on them, but the more experience they have in hiring the more they see how these traits can lead to problematic employees. These perceived traits come up in discussions with hiring managers, both when I start the search for candidates and when gathering feedback about why candidates are not moving forward. I have found these to be even more important at startup companies where the teams are smaller. Naturally, you cannot change your personality, but you should be self-aware enough not to project these traits.

Top personality traits that interviewers watch out for:

1. Overly self-absorbed.
2. Dishonest/untrustworthy.
3. Inability to take responsibility for mistakes, especially by blaming others.
4. Inflexible and not open to new ideas, suggestions, or coaching (I would include the "know-it-all" candidates in this category.).
5. Fragile ego that is unable to process constructive criticism.
6. Reckless risk taking (Calculated risk taking is great, but careless actions are not.).
7. Bitter/angry or anything else that might indicate a future toxic co-worker/employee.

I strongly recommend that you treat every interaction with any employee of the company as a type of interview. I have had candidates who did well in the interview with the hiring manager but did not get the job because the receptionist was asked what she thought of the applicant. There have also been candidates that I worked with that were doing great in the process, then let their professional guard down during a casual meeting and said something that was taken negatively. Every single interaction is something that may be part of the hiring decision.

How to Stand Out from Others

The employer's selection process is like a funnel, with numerous candidates entering at the top, and fewer progressing through each stage. As the interviews advance, the company must make decisions about you and your competition. At some point the company will gather feedback from all the people who interviewed you and hear their recommendations. To be the candidate offered the job, you need to make a lasting positive impression from the very beginning. It is often the small things that the interviewers remember that will separate an average candidate from the one who is offered the job.

First, try to understand the role that you are interviewing for beyond what is in the job ad. The requirements listed in an advertisement are the same as every other candidate reads. The more you understand about what makes someone an ideal hire for this role beyond what's in the ad, the better you will perform compared to other candidates. Ask your professional network as much as you can about what makes someone successful in that type of role, what type of personality that company typically hires, or any information you can gain about the department or hiring managers' personality. Do research online for articles, blogs, videos, or press releases related to what you are interviewing for. Also, as you go through the interview steps, stay curious and continue to learn about the company and people. Use this knowledge in your answers to demonstrate that you are not only a good fit for the known parts of the profile, but also a match for the aspects that are likely unknown to the other candidates.

During the interviews, try to establish personal connections with the interviewers. If you have any similarities with them, such as a shared background or interest, use that to your advantage. You might uncover these things through small talk with the interviewer, it might even be a passion for that type of work if you do not find anything on a personal level. Do this very nonchalantly or it will come across as insincere. Take notes after you are alone on the names of people you meet so that you can refer to them in the future.

Remember, your dream job is also someone else's dream. To stand out, you must do the small things that create a positive memory of your interactions with the company and its employees.

Here are a few things that will help you stand out:

Your interview will begin as soon as you arrive.
During job interviews, many companies request feedback from their front desk staff on the applicant's attitude. Be polite and professional with your behavior, tone, and body language. As soon as you get inside the building, be in interview mode.

Unique Value Proposition (U.V.P.).
Crafting a U.V.P. is a powerful tool to establish your personal candidate brand during an interview. It is a concise version of your response to the *"Tell me about yourself."* question, highlighting your top skills and attributes that overlap with the ideal profile. Your statement should be no longer than thirty seconds, or three to four sentences. This statement can serve as an introduction at job fairs or networking events, it also can be

used to start a conversation during an interview. You can also use it to support your other answers by providing examples of your skills. For more guidance on crafting an effective U.V.P. statement, refer to the companion workbook for this book.

Use the Answer/Ask technique.

The most exceptional candidates seem to be relaxed and confident, which I hope this book helps you with. In the typical interview scenario, there exists a one-sided dynamic: where the interviewer poses questions, and the candidate responds. However, the truly remarkable candidates go beyond mere responses; they engage in a polished, professional dialogue with the interviewer. A candidate capable of fostering such a back-and-forth exchange tends to leave a more impressive impression than those who simply furnish answers.

As mentioned earlier, mastering the Answer/Ask technique may require some practice, but it yields remarkable results when executed seamlessly, appearing entirely natural rather than intrusive. It's essential to avoid forcing the technique by interrupting the interviewer. Instead, aim to incorporate it organically by posing follow-up questions approximately thirty percent of the time after providing your responses. To refine this skill, consider practicing the Answer/Ask technique with a partner beforehand. Not only will this set you apart from most candidates, but it will also enhance your understanding of the job opportunity.

Example: Interviewer asks you *"Can you share your experience with patient record systems and any specific software tools you've used in your nursing career?"* and you respond with *"I've worked extensively with electronic health record systems such as Epic and Cerner. I've also used medication administration software like Meditech. How do you handle patient records in this hospital, and do you have any upcoming initiatives in this area?"*

Focus on your accomplishments more than your duties.

As I mentioned earlier in this book, there is a hierarchy to the answers you give. While a candidate may possess all the necessary skills for the job, providing weak answers can still leave a negative impression on the interviewer.

Use transferable skills.

If you do not have direct accomplishments or experience, use things that you have done that demonstrate the skills which will transfer well to the perfect candidate that they are seeking.

Forgive yourself if you make a mistake in the process.

Mistakes happen during interviews, but how you react to them can make all the difference. It's an opportunity to demonstrate resilience and composure in the face of adversity. It is essential to focus on the moment and not allow a mistake to ruin the rest of the meeting. This is a chance to show your ability to handle setbacks professionally and with confidence.

Closing statement.

As an interview is concluding, it is pivotal to make the last impression you leave with the interviewer a strong one. Thank them for their time, let them know that you enjoyed meeting them, express interest in the next step of the process, and give a one or two sentence summary of why you are a good match.

The advice in this chapter will allow you to make a positive impression on the interviewer by demonstrating your superior fit for the skills and characteristics that distinguish you from the others who are under consideration. To stand out in the interview process and be more successful, you will need to be specific and as genuine as possible in your answers. Avoid using rehearsed or monotone responses, as this will cause you to fade into the background and be easily forgotten. Additionally, refrain from over-exaggerating your skills and abilities.

Best Questions That Candidates Ask the Interviewer

Near the end of most interviews, you are usually asked if you have any questions for the interviewer. This is a fantastic opportunity to gain insights into whether the job is a good fit for your goals, showcase your suitability for the position, and refine your understanding of the ideal profile. Failing to ask questions gives the impression that you are not a serious candidate or are simply seeking any job that you can get.

To be successful you will need to ask good questions, as it is one of the critical ways you differentiate yourself from the other candidates. You can also incorporate questions throughout the interview using the Answer/Ask technique mentioned earlier. When asked about remaining questions, ask two or three of the most relevant ones. Below, I have listed some of the best questions that I have heard from candidates. Use these questions prior to your interview to compile a list of the seven to ten most relevant ones that you like, this way you should still have two or three at the end of the interview that were left unanswered. You can even save questions on your phone or on a piece of paper and refer to them during the interview. (Note that most companies will be the ones to bring up compensation. DO NOT ask about compensation at the beginning of an interview process, it shows that your priorities are wrong.)

I have broken down the best questions into four categories.

About the interviewer.

"What was your background before being hired here? How has that benefited you?"

"What do you love most about working here?"

"How would you describe your own management style?"

"Is this the career path that you envisioned for yourself when you got your start?"

"What do you wish you knew back when you were in my shoes?"

"Why did you decide to work here?"

Company culture.

"How would you describe the company culture here?"

"What type of employee has been most successful at this company?"

"What about employees that have not worked out here, why didn't they succeed?"

"What are new employees most surprised by in their first few months here?"

"Why do employees love to work here?"

"What type of hires do not last very long with your company?"

Interest in being successful with the company.

"What would you need me to focus on in the first month on the job?"

"What additional responsibilities can be gained over time in this role?"

"What has been the biggest challenge for this role in the past?"

"What are the biggest company goals for the next few years, and how does this position affect those goals?"

"What have people who reported to you in the past done to be successful?"

"What would I need to accomplish in the first year in this job for you to view me as a successful hire?"

"What do you want this role to accomplish in the first 90 days?"

"How will you measure success for me in this role?"

"What advice would you give to me in order for me to be successful in this role?"

"What have past employees done to become successful in this type of role here?"

"What are the biggest challenges that the company faces, and how can I help in this role?"

"Who is the company's biggest competitor, and what can I do in this role to help beat them?"

"What is the one trait that you have seen in people who have been very successful in this type of role?"

Due diligence.

"How would you explain this job in your own words?"

"What does the interview process look like?"

"Why is this position available?"

"How long has this position been open?" (If it has already been open a couple of months or longer, here is a follow-up: *"What seems to be missing from candidates you have interviewed so far?"*)

"What is your timeframe for hiring someone for this position?"

"What do you think the company's biggest accomplishments will be in the next few years?"

Closing for the offer.

"What skills or experience do you wish I had to make myself a better fit for this position?"

"What are the next steps in the process?"

"What can I clarify about my background to show you that I am the best fit for the job?"

"When would you need me to start?" (Subtle way to get them to picture hiring you)

"Is there anything in my skills or experience that you feel I am lacking compared to what you are looking for?"

Throughout the interview process and again at the end of it, the interviewers will meet with each other to discuss their impressions and recommendations about the candidates. The questions that you ask or don't ask can significantly impact their decision-making. This is something you should spend time on to get it right.

Do not ever say that you don’t have any questions when asked. Use the information that you gain from the answers you receive to make any small, needed changes for your next interview. Remember to be aware of the time and respect any indications that the interview is ending. Avoid continuing to ask questions if the interview is running late as that will make the interviewer impatient and leave them with a negative memory about you.

Employer Red Flags

If you follow the advice in this book and prepare for an interview it can help you become a stronger and more confident candidate. Another step to your success is to realize that while you do need to demonstrate what makes you the best match for the job, you also are evaluating the company.

Although this can be a dangerous analogy, I believe that the best way to view interviewing for a job is compare it to dating. At some point in our lives, we are all single and looking for a good match. The employer is like the single person who has determined what their dream match looks like, the person who they want to be in a serious relationship with. They are not determining if you are a good person or a bad person, they are simply trying to determine if you are a good fit for what they want.

Can you imagine going through a dating process where the evaluation is one-sided? It does not really happen like that, and the same is true for interviewing. Just as the employer has determined their dream match, you have an idea of what you are looking for in your next job opportunity. Don't be deceived by misleading positive impressions that could lead you into a bad or toxic work situation. It is especially important that you pay attention to red flags, those warnings that become apparent during the interview process.

Here are employer red flags for you to be extremely cautious of.

Asking you illegal interview questions.

The legality of questions that employers are allowed to ask varies by country and state. It is important to research and understand what can and cannot be asked where you and the employer are located. In the United States, for instance, you should not be asked at any time in an interview process about your age, religion, race, national origin, gender, marital status, or if you are or plan to become pregnant. In some states, questions about current compensation are also prohibited. U.S.

employers are allowed to ask if you are legally old enough to work at that job, if you are legally authorized to work in the country, and if you can physically perform the duties of the job.

When you are in an interview process and are asked a question that you believe to be prohibited by law, you should not be confrontational about it. If possible, you should first try to answer without providing information which is protected, because I would like to think that some inexperienced interviewers simply make mistakes. If they persist or if there is a pattern of illegal questions, you should wrap up your interview politely and leave. In most countries there is a governmental agency that you can follow up with if you feel it is necessary. The main point of this chapter is that this is one of those red flags you should not ignore. Asking illegal questions is a warning about what kind of employer they would be.

High employee turnover compared to others in the industry.

While some employers may experience temporary high employee turnover due to changes in management or strategy, it is important to be cautious of those with a history of frequent turnover. This may be a terrific opportunity for you on paper, so go ahead and interview but try to understand why they have this history.

Do some research on social media to see the difference between the number of current and previous employees. Look at how long the current employees have been with the company. If there are a high number of employees that have been there less than one year it is either due to rapid expansion which is great or due to high turnover, which is a big red flag.

The description of the job in the interview does not match the description in the ad or is very unclear.

This might be a classic bait-and-switch tactic that happens because an employer realizes that the actual job is not that attractive. If the description they give you during the interview is different from the job that was advertised, it's essential to question a few things. If they change the job description once, will they do it again in the future? How bad is the job if they cannot provide a clear description of it?

Negative atmosphere.

Pay close attention to the interaction between co-workers, especially if you are on-site for an interview. Take note of how many employees seem to like each other and appear to be happy working together. If the people who know best what it is like to work at that company do not seem like it makes them happy, you must recognize that this could be you soon.

Disrespectful of your time.

We all get busy sometimes, and I know there have been occasions in my career where I have been late for an interview. But I try to be respectful and apologetic for wasting the candidates' time who had to wait for me. Like I said earlier about how we assume that you as the candidate are at your best during the interview, so are the employers. If they do not respect you or the time that you are spending in the interview process enough to even apologize when they kept you waiting, you can expect them to treat you even worse after you are an employee. While there is no need to be impolite or overly sensitive if this happens, this behavior should warn you about the kind of culture you might experience if you accept the job.

Compensation does not match expectations.

When it comes to discussing compensation during the interview process, some companies will disclose the range at the beginning, while others will bring it up at the end. Part of your preparation should be to research what is being paid in the market for this type of job for someone with the same level of experience and education that you have. When a company has "champaign tastes, on a beer budget" when it comes to hiring employees, that is a culture where they will ask increasingly more of you as time goes on. Now, the exceptions to this concern are jobs where the greatest value to you is gaining experience, or a startup that might be below market on cash compensation but provide equity in the company that you believe to be fair.

Asking you to complete free work as part of the process.

Many interview processes include steps where you may be asked to complete some work to test your skill level. This work is usually a hypothetical exercise that is used simply as an evaluation tool. If a company asks you to complete a project that is part of their normal course of doing business and wants you to do it unpaid, that is a big red flag. If their culture is one where they think it is okay to get one or more job candidates to do work for them for free, then how do you think they are going to treat you as an employee?

Negative company reviews.

Before you go in for an interview, make sure to research reviews online and ask former employees of the company that are in your professional network. Keep in mind that disgruntled former employees often have a bias when writing those reviews, so use it more as a guide to things you should question rather than unimpeachable facts. Look for patterns where the same negative comments are made by multiple former employees. These patterns should be red flags, especially if they relate to your main concerns about the job or company. During your interview process, pay attention to things you see or hear that match those claims.

Ask about how you deal with working with difficult people.

You should be on alert if you are asked variations of this question multiple times during the interview process. Read between the lines of phrases like *"they have high standards"*, *"they're a perfectionist"*, or *"they take some getting used to"*. These are warnings that the role might come with a negative or toxic co-worker. Being asked this question once in an interview process is not by itself a huge red flag, but it should prompt you to ask follow-up questions. If you are asked a question like this, give your answer using the Answer/Ask technique to find out if you should expect to be dealing with difficult people in this role. Their answer to your question might reveal a big red flag.

They gossip about previous employees.

We all want to avoid being in a toxic workplace, but environments come from the people within them. Gossip is a very toxic behavior that often involves details that are not true and are simply meant to smear someone's reputation. If an interviewer engages in this behavior during an interview process, it is a sign that the company has a toxic culture. These are not people that I would trust enough to work with and risk that they will try to smear me one day. They are trying to make themselves look good to you by saying something bad about a person who used to sit where you are. It is very unprofessional and it's a huge red flag.

Back to the dating analogy, there are other similarities. Confident, sincere, non-arrogant, likable people tend to do better in both the dating and interview processes. From there, each individual employer has an ideal profile that they are looking for, and the process is about trying to determine if there is a good enough match to enter an employer/employee relationship.

As in dating, you will certainly regret it if you ignore red flags that show themselves during the evaluation stage. It is important to confidently present yourself as a good fit for the job, but also evaluate the employer to see if they are a good fit for you. Keep presenting yourself enthusiastically as a good match until you are certain that you do not want to work there. If you lose your focus on presenting yourself as a good match, they might eliminate you from the process. If you are asking legitimate questions professionally during the interview process, a good employer will see that as a sign that you are serious about a long-term working relationship, but only if you continue to show interest.

What to Expect from Different Interview Processes

Employers utilize a variety of interviewing formats, and some candidates can get distracted when they find themselves in a format that they did not expect. To demystify these different interview types, I am listing them below with details so that if you ever encounter any of them, you will be familiar, confident, and remain focused on your objective.

Interview formats.

1-on-1.

This is the type of interview that most people are familiar with. It is just you and the interviewer discussing your background and the opportunity. Most of the advice in this book can be applied directly to this type of interview.

1-on-1 sequential.

This is a process with a series of 1-on-1 interviews, where if you do well, you will move onto the next round of interviews. Again, most people are familiar with this format, but these processes often end with a final interview that could use one of the other formats.

Panel.

The panel interview is one of the most dreaded because it is easy to become intimidated by it. In these interviews there is one candidate and two or more interviewers meeting at the same time. I usually see between three and five interviewers on a panel. We do this to shorten the process, to make collaborative hiring decisions based on seeing and hearing the same things, and sometimes to train new interviewers. This can also be used when the candidate is asked to make a presentation to a group, usually the same interviewers from the 1-on-1 interviews. Make good eye contact with everyone on the panel, spending slightly more time with the interviewer who asked the question. After you leave, all the interviewers give their feedback on what they think of you as a good fit, so try to create as many advocates on the panel as possible.

Half/Full day.

Usually reserved for the final stage of an interview process, the half/full day of interviewing format allows multiple stakeholders to participate in the hiring decision. During this type of interview, you will typically meet with your potential manager, peers, human resources representatives, managers from other teams or departments, and the hiring manager's boss. I once had a great candidate do very well in the morning interviews and then perform poorly in the afternoon. Their energy fell off later in the day and they did not get the job offer. Pay attention to staying hydrated and eating or snacking as needed during these types of long arduous interviewing days. Be conscious of your energy level and enthusiasm in each interview.

Informal.

Mostly used in interviews for senior positions in the form of taking a candidate to lunch or dinner. However, an informal interview can be as simple as having a peer give you a tour of the facility or chat with you in the lobby. I have seen candidates let their guard down and forget that they are still being evaluated. You should be as relaxed and comfortable as possible during the interview process, but remain professional, positive, and focused on showing how you fit the ideal profile.

Phone.

While an initial phone screen is typically a part of most interview processes, it can be included at any point along the way. The great advantage of doing your interview over the phone is that the interviewer cannot see you. This allows you to have your notes, resume, job description, and profile in front of you during the interview. It might seem trivial but standing up and smiling while you are talking on the phone does make a much better impression. Your voice will tend to project more confidently and friendlier. Immediately after you get off your phone call (or video call) you should jot down notes about the conversation while everything is still fresh in your memory. Notes about comments the interviewer made that give you more insight into the job duties, company culture, or any other comment that leads to a better understanding of the profile they are looking for will give you an advantage as you prepare for future interviews.

Video.

These interviews are becoming increasingly more common, video interviews have had a bit of a learning curve for some candidates. These are of course where you speak with the interviewer over Zoom, TEAMS, Google Meet, Skype, or something similar. I have had candidates make the mistake of keeping their cameras turned off during the interview. It is crucial to treat a video interview like an in-person meeting by dressing professionally and always keeping your camera turned on unless you have a technical issue. Many video conferencing platforms offer virtual backgrounds, which should be used if your physical background is distracting. I have also interviewed candidates who made the mistake of having their camera pointed towards the side of their computer screen, making it appear as though I was talking to their ear. Before any video interview, test that both your video and audio are working properly and be sure to direct the camera where you can give the impression of making eye contact with the interviewer.

One-way video application.

Some companies have begun using pre-recorded video answers to screening questions as part of the application process. In addition to the advice that I gave for video interviews, you should uncover the details of the settings for that video application. Some will allow you to record a video as many times as you want before submitting it, while others will have a limit. With formats that limit the times that you can record, you can practice your answers using your smartphone before recording in the application itself.

Peer.

These interviews can be in a formal 1-on-1, panel, video, or casual setting. Being interviewed by a potential future co-worker allows you to gain insights from a unique perspective, but it is full of pitfalls. Some candidates fail because they act too casual when speaking with a peer, resulting in giving negative answers or asking inappropriate questions that they would not ask the hiring manager. To be successful in your interview process you need to remember that you are always being evaluated and the peer will be asked about their interaction with you.

Stress.

If you are interviewing for a job that will require you to deal with stressful situations, then it is a good idea for the employer to find out how you handle yourself under stress. When I have used this technique, I typically change my tone of voice and act more aggressively towards the candidate, but the stress interviews can take on different forms. At the very least you should expect to be asked uncomfortable or stressful questions that are meant to emulate the type of stress in this job. The most successful preparation is to do enough research to know whether you can expect a stress interview. Being surprised by these types of interviews increases the chances of failure. If you do recognize that you are being tested on how you handle stress, try to think about the perfect candidate that they are trying to hire and do what you can to demonstrate how your responses make you a match. When you are researching the company, do a search with the company name and "Stress Interview" to see if this is something you should expect.

Group.

These are interviews with a group of candidates, meeting with one to a few interviewers at once. I am not a huge fan of this type of interview as its greatest value is to simply weed candidates out quickly. The interviewer(s) will gather multiple candidates together and make a presentation about the job opportunity, which is usually not the most attractive job. They will then instruct anyone who is not interested in the role to please leave. They will usually then conduct 1-on-1 interviews with those remaining interested candidates. There is not much advice I can give for you to perform well in this type of interview, as it is more about you deciding if you like what they tell you about the job. Just make sure that you ask questions and understand the role. The reason they usually use a group interview is because many candidates in the past have rejected the job, and you should ask yourself why.

The Job Offer

After successfully completing the interview process, you may have an offer of employment coming your way. Although companies typically initially make verbal offers, many will follow that up with a written offer letter. You can expect that your offer will have an expiration date because the employer needs to move onto their next choice if you don't accept the job. One week is the standard time frame for an offer to expire and while you can negotiate this deadline, if you ask for two or more weeks it may suggest that the offer is not your top choice. It comes across as being back in high school asking someone to the prom and their response is that they want to give you an answer next month. This is someone hoping for a better offer before they have to give you their decision. Like anyone else, hiring managers usually don't want to be someone's backup plan so be cautious with this negotiation.

While most candidates do not negotiate their job offers, we are not offended when they try. We can be very unhappy by the way that some candidates do it.

Negotiating the details of a job offer is more successful if you have followed the advice in this book and shown the employer that you are a high-value candidate. Salary is also not the only aspect of an offer that you can negotiate. Depending on the company, you can request better shifts, equity in the company, education or training reimbursement, more responsibilities to gain experience, and other details of the offer.

For additional detailed information on successful salary negotiation, please read ***SoaringME.com Guide to Successful Salary Negotiation.*** Be cautious when seeking other advice as I have seen some horrible opinions given by people who portray themselves as an expert but who simply do not know what they are talking about.

When asked about your salary expectations, avoid staying silent as some suggest. It is simply not true that "the last one to speak wins". Playing these types of negotiation games may work for you in some limited cases despite your use of them, not because of it. If an employer wants to hire you, they might overlook their concerns about this type of behavior. However, most of the time, playing negotiation games will make you appear misguided or untrustworthy.

You will have a higher success rate with a professional approach. Instead of games, be prepared to answer the question about your expectations and know what a fair and realistic market price is for the services you are offering. Salary is the price at which you are willing to sell your labor to an employer who is willing to pay that amount for what they are getting in return. The most successful salary negotiators know what a fair and realistic market price is for their services.

If you have found value in this book, please take a moment to leave a rating and inform others.

Visit SoaringME.com or ask your favorite bookstore for our other books to help your career.

About the Author

M.L. Miller was born in Goldendale, Washington, raised in Oregon, and has since lived in various locations across America. Currently, he and his wife Wilawan divide their time between the United States and Thailand.

Having studied Economics/Finance at the University of Hartford in Connecticut, M.L. began a career in recruitment in

1997, working for hundreds of client companies from Fortune 100 large corporations to start-ups. During this time, he has conducted somewhere between twenty and thirty thousand job interviews and has hired thousands of employees in a variety of roles from entry-level to C-Suite and Board-Level. During his career he managed a corporate recruiting team, increasing their hires by over thirty-three percent in under two years. He started Ethical Recruiters, Inc., an executive recruitment firm and later SoaringME, a company that educates candidates on how to be more successful in job interviewing.

Within this framework, M.L. has also published several books related to the subject:

SoaringME The Ultimate Guide to Successful Job Searching.

SoaringME The Ultimate Guide to Successful Job Interviewing.

SoaringME COMPANION WORKBOOK The Ultimate Guide to Successful Job Interviewing.

SoaringME.com: Guide to Successful Salary Negotiation.

He also has several Ultimate Guides on interviewing for specific careers.

In his free time, M.L. is an avid cyclist and has ridden the annual 200-mile Seattle-to-Portland bike ride five times so far. He also enjoys traveling domestically and internationally.

M.L. has worked with homeless military veterans for a couple of years through a non-profit organization. He used his experience to help them improve interviewing skills, write resumes, and obtain employment to get back on their feet. He also raises money for children's mental health charities.

In the future, M.L. plans to continue his career in talent acquisition. His personal goal is to one day combine his love of cycling and travel to complete 100-mile bike rides on five different continents.

His favorite quote is "Every strike brings me closer to the next home run." – Babe Ruth.

Made in United States
Orlando, FL
04 November 2026

90201197R00095